POC

INSECTS

OF EAST AFRICA

DINO J. MARTINS

Published by Struik Nature
(an imprint of Penguin Random House South Africa (Pty) Ltd)
Reg. No. 1953/000441/07
The Estuaries No. 4, Oxbow Crescent, Century Avenue, Century City, 7441
PO Box 1144, Cape Town, 8000 South Africa

www.penguinrandomhouse.co.za

First published in 2014

3 5 7 9 10 8 6 4

Copyright © in text, 2015: Dino Martins
Copyright © in photographs, 2015: Dino Martins
(unless otherwise indicated alongside image)
Copyright © in maps, 2015: Chris and Mathilde Stuart
Copyright © in published edition, 2015: Penguin Random House South Africa (Pty) Ltd

Publishing manager: Pippa Parker
Managing editor: Helen de Villiers
Editor: Emily Bowles
Designer: Gillian Black
Reproduction by Hirt & Carter Cape (Pty) Ltd
Printed and bound by Toppan Leefung Packaging and Printing
(Dongguan) Co., Ltd., China

Penguin Random House is committed to a sustainable future
for our business, our readers and our planet. This book is made from
Forest Stewardship Council® certified paper.

All rights reserved. No part of this publication may be reproduced, stored in a retrieval
system or transmitted, in any form or by any means, electronic, mechanical, photocopying,
recording or otherwise, without the prior written permission of the copyright owner(s).

ISBN 978 1 77007 894 9. E-PUB 978 1 77584 272 9. E-PDF 978 1 77584 273 6.

Front cover photograph: Green tachinid fly. Back cover photographs (top to bottom): Burnet moth, black sugar ant, water penny (F. Smith), honeybee and dark blue pansy (M.N. Mutiso). Title page photograph: Picasso bugs. Page 3 photograph: Praying mantis.

ACKNOWLEDGEMENTS

This book is inspired by and dedicated to the many young naturalists, students and communities
that I have had the pleasure of training and working with in East Africa. I have been able to
develop my work on insects through collaboration and support from many different institutions
over the years including Nature Kenya, the National Museums of Kenya, the Turkana Basin
Institute, the Museum of Comparative Zoology at Harvard University, the Kenya Horticultural
Society, the Mpala Research Centre, the Kenya Agricultural Research Institute, the Kenya Wildlife
Society, the Pest Control Products Board, the Suyian Trust, the National Geographic Society and
the Food and Agricultural Organisation of the United Nations (FAO).
    Information, insights, support, and collaboration in many different forms have been provided
by: A. Powys, G. Powys, L. Coverdale, D. Roberts, N. Pierce, D. Haig, A. Pringle, F. Jenkins,
W. Tong, J. Kingdon, L. Snook, D. Estes, E.O. Wilson, K. Horton, R. Leakey, M. Leakey, L. Leakey,
G. Domberger, D. Wallis, E. Whitley, A . Whitley, I. Angelei, P. Kahumbu, S. Kahumbu, B. Gemmill-
Herren, H. Herren, S. Miller, T. Kuklenski-Miller, R. Copeland, W. Kinuthia, L. Njoroge, C. Hemp,
I. Gordon, M. Kasina, S. Kocher, M. Kinnaird, J. Mamlin, S.E. Mamlin, N. Croze, E. Krystall, V. Otieno,
P. Matiku, D. Kathurima, F. Ng'weno, M. Gikungu, T. Griswold, L. Packer, B. Danforth, C. Eardley,
M. Kulhmann, J. Ascher, N. Azzu, P. Lomosingo, B. Obanda, T. Achevi, W. Okeka, W. Tiren,
J. Wakhungu, J. Margaret, C. Zook, J. Sandhu, P.D. Paterson, and many, many others. I am
especially thankful to M.N. Mutiso, E.M. Gitonga, A. Powys and F. Smith for the use of their photos.
    I am very grateful for the support from Struik Nature, and especially Pippa Parker, for taking
on this project and publishing this work on East African insects.

CONTENTS

INTRODUCTION

Over 1 million species of insect have been described; this truly is one of the most wonderful, interesting and diverse groups of creatures on our planet. These amazing organisms can be found almost everywhere in East Africa, from the snow-capped peaks of mounts Kenya and Kilimanjaro to the hottest, driest deserts and in every imaginable habitat in between. Insects live in the soil, inside both dead and living wood, in water, on every possible plant part and even on or in the bodies of animals (including humans!).

There is no other group of organisms that has such an immense daily impact on human lives and livelihoods. Insects are essential for the functioning of virtually all East African ecosystems: they play a vital role in recycling nutrients and energy, breaking down biomass, building and aerating soil, dispersing seeds and pollinating plants. For example, over 80 per cent of all flowering plants depend on insects for pollination. Without bees and other insect pollinators there would be no mangoes, avocados, guavas, apples, pears, plums, papaya, passion fruit, cowpeas or cocoa (chocolate) – and far less coffee would be available in East Africa! In just one area of Kenya alone (Baringo County), bee pollination of watermelons is worth over $10 million per year. It is estimated that we owe one in three bites of food to the services of pollinators, mainly insects.

Insects are also responsible for much damage to crops. Locusts, armyworms, aphids, whiteflies and many other pest species take a toll on crops across East Africa. Maize weevils, and other insects that feed on stored grains, impose a heavy tax on our harvests by eating four out of every 10 bags harvested. However, one of the best ways of controlling pests is by encouraging their natural predators and parasites, and many insects themselves feed voraciously on insect pest species, providing efficient natural pest control.

Insects are also important vectors of disease in East Africa, with various species of mosquito transmitting malaria, lymphatic filariasis (elephantiasis) and yellow fever (now very rare), and tsetse flies transmitting sleeping sickness to humans and nagana (trypanosomiasis) to livestock. Other insect parasites

A leafcutter bee approaches a flowering pigeon pea – insects are among the most important wild pollinators.

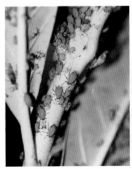

Milkweed aphids clustered on Gomphocarpus stenophylla

include jiggers (a kind of flea), which cause much suffering, especially among children in rural areas. The infamous 'Nairobi Eye' (caused by a species of rove beetle) erupts seasonally and plagues people across East Africa with severe, painful blisters.

Many insects are exploited for food in East Africa, including termites and various grasshoppers and locusts, which are considered a delicacy in some areas. Beautiful butterflies are reared for export and display in live butterfly houses by a number of rural communities in East Africa, providing an essential source of income and an impetus to conserve forest habitats.

Delicious termite alates for sale in the market at Kakamega Town, Western Kenya

This book is meant to serve as an introduction to the amazing insect diversity of East Africa. With just over 400 species described, this is just a drop in the ocean of insect diversity, but hopefully it will inspire more interest, awareness and appreciation of these fascinating, strange and wonderful creatures.

Insect classification

Insects are grouped together in the class Insecta. They have existed on the earth for many hundreds of millions of years. Insects are part of the phylum Arthropoda (animals with jointed limbs and segmented bodies), which includes the millipedes, spiders, scorpions and others. Insects are thought to have diversified and co-evolved together with the majority of flowering plants (angiosperms). Evolutionary studies of insects indicate that they have ruled the planet for a long time; therefore, we are actually living in the 'Age of Insects'!

A fulvous hawkmoth frequenting Combretum *flowers*

The zig-zag fruit chafer beetle well illustrates the striking beauty of many insects.

All living things that have been formally described by the science of taxonomy (classification) can be placed in a taxonomic hierarchy. Comparing honeybees and humans allows us to better understand how this is organised.

Firstly, all bees (and other insects) and all humans (and other animals) share the same kingdom: the Animalia (animals). Moving another step along the hierarchy takes us into the level of phlya (singular: phylum). This is where humans and honeybees diverge: humans are in the phylum Chordata (the animals with backbones/spinal columns) and honeybees are in the phylum Arthropoda (the animals with jointed limbs).

A safari ant (also known as a driver ant) in a defensive posture

Another step takes us to the class level. Humans are Mammalia (whose defining features include nurturing young with milk from mammary glands, hairy bodies and embryonic development in a womb), while honeybees are in the class Insecta (six legs, segmented bodies organised into three main parts). Next we come to the order level. Here, humans are part of the order Primates, while honeybees are part of the order Hymenoptera (which includes all the ants, bees and wasps).

Another step takes us to the family level. Humans are Hominids, and honeybees are in the family Apidae. Several different families of bees occur in East Africa. Some of these are further organised into subfamilies, tribes and other levels of organisation.

Each family is further broken down to the level of the genus. Humans are in the genus *Homo*, and honeybees are in the genus *Apis*. **Most of the insect entries featured in this book are presented at the family or genus level, as we simply don't know much about most of the next level, that of species, in East Africa. Closely related groups and species appear together.**

The final level of classification is that of the species. What is a species? The basic definition of a biological species is a population within which individuals can reproduce with each other. Humans bear the species name *sapiens*, which means 'wise', while honeybees are *mellifera*, meaning 'nectar-loving'.

	Honeybee	Human
Kingdom	Animalia	Animalia
Phylum	Arthropoda (animals with jointed limbs)	Chordata (animals with backbones)
Class	Insecta	Mammalia
Order	Hymenoptera	Primates
Family	Apidae	Hominidae
Genus	*Apis*	*Homo*
Species	*mellifera* ('nectar-loving')	*sapiens* ('wise')

The antennae of this male emperor moth enable it to detect female pheromones.

A carpenter bee visiting a flowering Crotolaria *in northern Kenya*

Insect anatomy

Insects have a distinctive body structure divided into segments. They have an exoskeleton made from chitin, a hard, but flexible, waterproof substance. There are three main parts to the insect body: head, thorax and abdomen. The head carries the eyes, mouth and antennae. Most insects have one pair of compound eyes. Antennae vary in shape and length, but are important sensory organs. Insect mouthparts are highly variable, depending on the species and how it is adapted to feeding.

A bluebottle fly feeding from a Euphorbia *flower using its extended proboscis*

Insect parts (as shown on a milkweed locust)

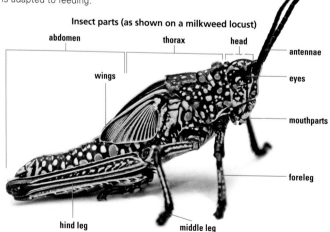

abdomen · thorax · head · antennae · eyes · mouthparts · foreleg · wings · hind leg · middle leg

A Tephritid fruit fly with colourful eyes

A young milkweed locust suns itself on a leaf.

The thorax is the middle section of the insect's body. It bears the legs and the wings, if they are present. Legs are variable and may be built for running, jumping, grabbing prey, digging, swimming or walking on water, among many other adaptations. The abdomen is the 'back end' of the insect's body, and is often longer, with softer segments. It contains the digestive and reproductive organs. In some species there are obvious appendages projecting from the abdomen, including ovipositors in females, which are used for laying eggs.

Insect life cycles: metamorphosis

Insects may complete their life cycle by undergoing either incomplete or complete metamorphosis. Incomplete or gradual metamorphosis entails three different stages: first an **egg** stage, then a feeding stage when the immature **larva** or **nymph** grows larger, and finally a **mature adult** (reproductive) stage. Grasshoppers, crickets, locusts, all of the true bugs, dragonflies, termites and mayflies are examples of insects with this kind of life cycle. By contrast, complete metamorphosis has four distinct stages: the **egg**, then the **larval stage** focused on feeding and growth, followed by a **pupal stage** (when no feeding occurs) during which the grub-like larva undergoes an amazing transformation, and finally the **mature adult** (reproductive) stage. All true flies, beetles, ants, bees, wasps, butterflies and moths have this kind of life cycle.

Area covered by this guide

The range of this book encompasses Uganda, Kenya, Tanzania, Rwanda and Burundi. The following is a simplified vegetation map, showing the main vegetation zones that occur across this region. Insect diversity is closely tied to plant diversity in East Africa. The forest zones are among the richest areas for insect life. Grasslands and drylands are important, too, especially following seasonal rains. Many vegetation zones that are isolated in higher altitude areas have become 'islands', and insect species occurring here are often endemic or localised (have a narrow geographical distribution).

East African vegetation

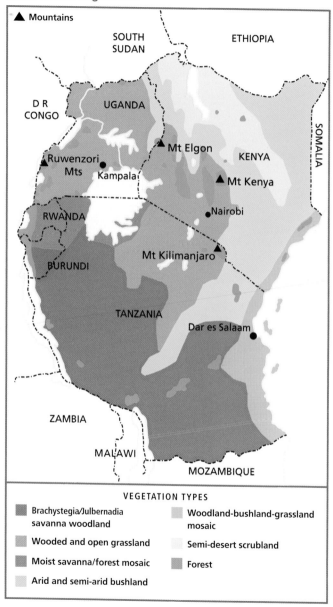

VEGETATION TYPES

- Brachystegia/Julbernadia savanna woodland
- Wooded and open grassland
- Moist savanna/forest mosaic
- Arid and semi-arid bushland
- Woodland-bushland-grassland mosaic
- Semi-desert scrubland
- Forest

How to use this book

The species in this book include those that are frequently encountered, ecologically important or that are simply noticeable. This guide presents just a first, tiny glimpse of the diversity, ecology and natural history of East Africa's insects.

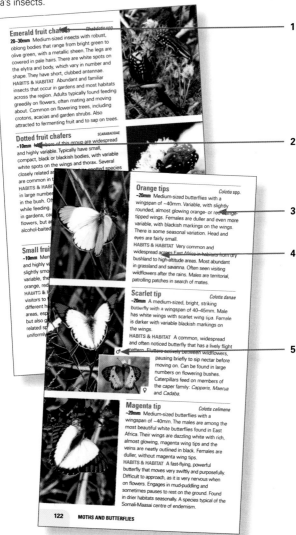

1

Emerald fruit chafers — *Rhabdotis* spp.

20–30mm Medium-sized insects with robust, oblong bodies that range from bright green to olive green, with a metallic sheen. The legs are covered in pale hairs. There are white spots on the elytra and body, which vary in number and shape. They have short, clubbed antennae.

HABITS & HABITAT Abundant and familiar insects that occur in gardens and most habitats across the region. Adults typically found feeding greedily on flowers, often mating and moving about. Common on flowering trees, including crotons, acacias and garden shrubs. Also attracted to fermenting fruit and to sap on trees.

2

Dotted fruit chafers — SCARABAEIDAE

~10mm Members of this group are widespread and highly variable. Typically have small, compact, black or blackish bodies, with variable white spots on the wings and thorax. Several closely related and [...] spotted species are common in [...]

HABITS & HABIT[...] in large number[...] in the bush. Of[...] while feeding[...] in gardens, ca[...] flowers, but a[...] alcohol-baited [...]

Small frui[...]

~10mm Mem[...] and highly va[...] slightly smo[...] variable, the[...] orange, red[...]

HABITS & [...] visitors to [...] different h[...] areas, esp[...] but also [...] related sp[...] uniformly[...]

Orange tips — *Colotis* spp.

~20mm Medium-sized butterflies with a wingspan of ~40mm. Variable, with slightly rounded, almost glowing orange- or red-orange-tipped wings. Females are duller and even more variable, with blackish markings on the wings. There is some seasonal variation. Head and eyes are fairly small.

3

HABITS & HABITAT Very common and widespread across East Africa in habitats from dry bushland to high-altitude areas. Most abundant in grassland and savanna. Often seen visiting wildflowers after the rains. Males are territorial, patrolling patches in search of mates.

4

Scarlet tip — *Colotis danae*

~20mm A medium-sized, bright, striking butterfly with a wingspan of 40–45mm. Male has white wings with scarlet wing tips. Female is darker with variable blackish markings on the wings.

HABITS & HABITAT A common, widespread and noticed butterfly that has a lively flight pattern. Flutters actively between wildflowers, pausing briefly to sip nectar before moving on. Can be found in large numbers on flowering bushes. Caterpillars feed on members of the caper family: *Capparis*, *Maerua* and *Cadaba*.

♂

♀

5

Magenta tip — *Colotis celimene*

~20mm Medium-sized butterflies with a wingspan of ~40mm. The males are among the most beautiful white butterflies found in East Africa. Their wings are dazzling white with rich, almost glowing, magenta wing tips and the veins are neatly outlined in black. Females are duller, without magenta wing tips.

HABITS & HABITAT A fast-flying, powerful butterfly that moves very swiftly and purposefully. Difficult to approach, as it is very nervous when on flowers. Engages in mud-puddling and sometimes pauses to rest on the ground. Found in drier habitats seasonally. A species typical of the Somali-Maasai centre of endemism.

122   MOTHS AND BUTTERFLIES

1 **NAME:** As far as possible, the common English name is given first, as it is often confusing for non-scientists to decipher scientific names. Depending on the classification level of the the particular species entry, a family or order name (in small caps), the name of the genus (in italics) or the full species name (a two-part italicised name) is also supplied.

2 **SIZE:** An estimated length from 'nose to tail' is presented. This measurement is from the tip of the insect's head to the end of its abdomen. Wingspans, where known, are presented as a separate measurement for butterflies and moths.

   As most insects are small creatures, size is a relative measure. Within each group of insects size can vary greatly; for example, East Africa is home to the world's heaviest beetles, goliath beetles, but most beetles are much smaller.

The following are the general size guidelines used in this book:

   Tiny/minute: these are very small insects, usually 1–2mm

   Small: under 5mm

   Medium: 5–25mm

   Large: over 25mm

   Note that if an insect is unusually large or small for its group, this is stated in the text. Size varies naturally and may depend on the quantity of food that an insect has had access to, the temperature during its development, and its sex. In addition, not all insects have been well studied. For these reasons, we have presented the average size for some species, while for others a range is given.

3 **DESCRIPTION:** A brief description of the insect is given, including its size, colour, shape and any other distinctive features that may aid identification. Note that as many insects in this book are discussed at the family or genus level, these descriptions are meant to be broad guidelines only.

4 **HABITS & HABITAT:** This is a general discussion of where a particular insect is found, outlining some of its behaviour and providing a brief overview of the roles it might play (for example, if it is a pollinator, pest or parasite).

5 Occasionally male ♂ or female ♀ insects are indicated.

NOTE: So little is known about most of our insects in East Africa that there is plenty of scope for the public to become involved. Observations, photographs and records of insects shared by the general public and amateur naturalists make an important contribution to our wider understanding and knowledge of what is happening in the field, especially in today's changing world. If you have any questions, comments, or requests for identification, please get in touch via the Insect Committee of Nature Kenya:
insects.eanhs@gmail.com or **insects@naturekenya.org**, or write to:
Dr Dino J. Martins, Insect Committee of Nature, P O Box 44486, GPO 00100 Nairobi, Kenya.

Springtails COLLEMBOLA

1–2mm Very tiny, soft-bodied, wingless creatures that are related to insects. They are typically grey, white, pale orange or yellow. Some species have eyes while others are eyeless. All springtails have short antennae.
HABITS & HABITAT The name refers to their ability to jump using a specialised organ on their undersides called a furcula. They do this when disturbed or threatened. Widespread and abundant in moist habitats in soil, leaf litter, pools and puddles, rotting logs and compost heaps. Biology poorly known.

Silverfish THYSANURA

5–15mm Very ancient, primitive insects with soft, flat bodies. Eyes are separated on the head, and are sometimes absent. When active, silverfish vigorously twitch their long antennae. The body is covered in metallic scales that readily rub off when touched.
HABITS & HABITAT Most familiar are the domestic species that live in houses among books and clothing, where they can cause damage. They feed on dry organic matter and can survive without drinking water, as they can absorb moisture directly from the air. Some species live in ant and termite nests. Mostly nocturnal.

Mayfly nymphs EPHEMEROPTERA

5–25mm Mayfly nymphs are the aquatic immature larval stage of the adult winged mayflies that are often drawn to lights. They are similar to dragonfly larvae, but can be distinguished by the gills on the sides of their bodies.
HABITS & HABITAT Mayfly larvae are active insects that occur in streams, lakes and other freshwater bodies, where they move around in litter and rocks. They feed on detritus, including leaves and other fine organic matter. **Flat-headed mayfly** larvae (pictured here) often cling to rocks.

Mayfly adults

EPHEMEROPTERA

5–35mm Adult mayflies are delicate insects that typically live for a few hours at most. They have elongated, cylindrical bodies, two pairs of flimsy wings and 2–3 'tails' on the abdomen. Colouring is typically pale grey, ivory, light brown or tan. **HABITS & HABITAT** Mayflies are most often observed when attracted to lights in the evening and at night. They sometimes gather in large numbers during their brief mating flights. Adults can also be found floating on the surfaces of ponds and water bodies the morning after mating flights.

E.M. GITONGA

Swamp bluets

Africallagma spp.

25–30mm Elegant, classic damselflies. Males have unmistakable but variable bright sky blue and black markings on the body. Females are dull tan and dark brown with black. Both sexes tiny, but size is variable in these damselflies. **HABITS & HABITAT** Common and widespread across all suitable habitats in East Africa. Found near dams, ponds, pools, swamps and slow flowing streams with plenty of reeds or sedges on which to perch. Ubiquitous in suitable habitats, they can be among the most abundant species of damselfly encountered seasonally.

A. POWYS

Common bluetail

Ischnura senegalensis

25–30mm A dainty, elegant damselfly that can be variable in colouring depending on age and sex. Males are black with green stripes and a blue patch at the tip of the abdomen. Females are duller, sometimes with orange legs and thorax. **HABITS & HABITAT** A common and familiar species that occurs all over East Africa near to ponds, pools and swamps and in mildly saline and alkaline habitats such as wetlands in the Great Rift Valley. Favours calm, still water. Can be very common seasonally, especially at the beginning of the rains.

A. POWYS

Dancing jewel
Platycypha caligata

~35mm One of East Africa's most distinctive, recognisable and beautiful insects. Males are unmistakable with their blue abdomens, gold-orange markings on the thorax and red-and-white legs. Females are dull brown and grey.
HABITS & HABITAT Can be found in the vicinity of flowing, unpolluted streams in warm areas throughout East Africa. Males perch on twigs and rocks and perform courtship dances in patches of sunlight for shy females that perch in more secluded spots.

Ruby jewels
Chlorocypha spp.

~35mm Gorgeous jewel damselflies. Males have a distinctive smouldering ruby red abdomen that is especially eye-catching in sunlight. Eyes are black and bulging. Females are much duller – brown, with paler markings.
HABITS & HABITAT Shy, localised and retiring jewel damselflies of rainforest streams and heavily wooded areas in western Kenya, western Tanzania, Uganda, Rwanda and Burundi. Males are territorial and will spend long periods of time in an area, returning frequently to perches in the vicinity.

Glistening demoiselle
Phaon iridipennis

~75mm A large and distinctive damselfly that appears somewhat dull when viewed from a distance on its typically shaded perches. However, wings flash iridescent mauve when it flits past in sunlight. Female slightly smaller and duller than male.
HABITS & HABITAT A relatively common and widespread species that is found at low altitudes along major rivers in coastal and woodland areas. Prefers to perch in shaded spots and can be nervous and difficult to approach. Sometimes gregarious and found in small numbers.

Spreadwings LESTIDAE

~40mm A widespread group of damselflies whose members are distinguished at rest by the way they hold their wings open at a slight angle. Males are typically marked with green or yellow and black. Females are pale beige or light brown.

HABITS & HABITAT Spreadwings are localised damselflies associated with seasonal wetlands. Common around ponds, pools and small swamps that fill with rain. Males can often be found holding onto females. This is mate-guarding behaviour intended to keep other males from cuckolding them.

Sapphire *Umma sapphirina*

~70mm One of the most distinctive and beautiful of East Africa's damselflies. Body is metallic with gorgeous, reflective, emerald green colouring that can shift to blue-green or shining sapphire depending on the prevailing light.

HABITS & HABITAT A shy and retiring species found along streams in the rainforests of western Kenya, Uganda, Rwanda and Burundi. Frequently found hawking insects from a perch that it returns to. Sapphires are often noticed when startled along a trail: they fly past in a bright flash of iridescent colour.

Common citrils *Ceriagrion* spp.

40–45mm One of the most familiar and recognisable damselflies of East Africa. The males have bright orange abdomens and yellow-orange heads with distinctively contrasting green eyes. Females are dull greenish-grey and dark-eyed.

HABITS & HABITAT Very common and widespread across East Africa near dams, ponds, pools, swamps and the sheltered edges of slow-flowing streams and rivers. Often found in camps and lodges or in gardens with ponds. Flutters weakly when startled, retiring to perch on a sheltered spot among vegetation.

Acacia sprite *Pseudagrion acaciae*

30–35mm A small, dainty damselfly with bright red eyes and face. Body black with green and blue markings or bands. Females much duller, with greenish-brown markings on the body and head.

HABITS & HABITAT Very common at fairly low altitude along rivers and slow-flowing streams, including in areas at the foot of mountain ranges in northern Kenya and Uganda. Perches on rocks, twigs and debris. The similar and related Maasai Sprite can be found at dams, ponds and other wetlands.

Cherry-eyed sprites *Pseudagrion* spp.

35–40mm One of several species of damselfly with red eyes (the shade and intensity of the red varies between species). Males are typically black with bluish and greenish markings on the body. Females usually have far duller colouring.

HABITS & HABITAT Both sexes can be found perching and fluttering at the edges of dams, ponds, pools, swamps, slow-flowing streams and rivers with fringing vegetation. Males often hover over the water while courting females or harassing other couples that have paired up.

Whisps *Agriocnemis* spp.

18–22mm The smallest and daintiest of the East African damselflies. Delicately built. Males are very brightly coloured with orange, red and blue markings, and the tips of their abdomens are especially vivid. Females have dull colouring.

HABITS & HABITAT Can be very common and gregarious at the edges of still water, including slow-flowing, vegetated streams, ponds, dams, wetlands and seasonally flooded grassland areas. Flight weak and fluttering. They return frequently to the safety of their perches.

Hooktails
Paragomphus spp.

40–45mm A common and widespread group of dragonflies whose distinctive feature is the abdomen, which has a large, inflated, hooked tip. Males and females are similar, with green markings on a darker body. Males are more brightly marked and have narrower abdomens than do the females.

HABITS & HABITAT Common and widespread around water bodies fringed with sand and where they can perch on sunny rocks. Can be gregarious, but also found singly in dry season, sometimes in bush far from water.

Tigertail
Ictinogomphus ferox

70–95mm One of the most striking dragonflies of the region. Large, with boldly striped black-and-yellow markings on the abdomen and body and a slightly inflated tail tip. Males and females are similar in patterning and coloration.

HABITS & HABITAT A widespread species that is found in open savanna and grassland areas along rivers or near open, still or moving water bodies. They often perch on prominent twigs or branches from where they make flights and to which they return periodically. They lift their abdomens skyward in hot weather.

M N. MUTISO

Blue emperor
Anax imperator

80–90mm A brightly coloured, active and distinctive dragonfly. Males have bright blue on the abdomen and green on the head, eyes and thorax. Females are green, with some brown markings on the abdomen.

HABITS & HABITAT Among the most engaging dragonflies to watch on safari, emperors, including the related red emperor and black emperor, are strong fliers, move swiftly and soar over water, grassy verges and surrounding open areas. They hang suspended from twigs or stems when resting.

Yellowjacks
Notogomphus spp.

50–55mm A group of quite uniformly marked dragonflies that have a stripe running down the length of the body. Typically dark with green or greenish-yellow markings. Males and females have similar colouring.

HABITS & HABITAT These dragonflies are found in forest and woodland areas, where they frequent rivers and streams, moving swiftly up and down through the forest. Can be common. Related Maathai's clubtail (*Notogomphus maathaiae*) was recently discovered and named in honour of Kenyan Nobel laureate Wangari Maathai.

Red-veined dropwing
Trithemis arteriosa

~35mm Among the most familiar and charming of East African dragonflies. Males are distinguished by their black-tipped, bright red abdomens. Can be separated from similar species by the narrow build and the red veins in the wings. Females are dull yellow-brown and black and can be variable.

HABITS & HABITAT Among the most abundant and widespread of all East African dragonflies, they can be found around wetlands, streams, rivers, lakes and ponds throughout the region, from coastal to highland areas.

Violet dropwing
Trithemis annulata

~35mm Very distinctive and beautiful dragonflies. Males have a unique plum-coloured body with a soft iridescence and seem to glow in the sunlight. Females are dull olive brown to grey.

HABITS & HABITAT Common and widespread in the warm areas of East Africa, where they are found on the margins of most lakes (including L. Turkana, L. Victoria and other freshwater lakes) and their associated rivers, ponds and wetlands. They often perch on vegetation close to or overhanging water.

Pintail
Acisoma panorpoides

25–30mm A small and pretty species. Males have blue-green eyes and a distinctly tapering abdomen, hence the name 'pintail'. A dark stripe runs down the blue abdomen. Females are dull with a similar stripe.

HABITS & HABITAT Common and widespread at wetlands (especially flooded areas with lush vegetation such as sedges) in warm grassland, bush and savanna habitats. They raise their abdomens skyward in hot weather and spend long periods perched on vegetation.

Black-tailed skimmer
Nesciothemis farinosa

40–45mm A distinctive and noticeable dragonfly species. Males are pale powdery blue with a contrasting black abdomen that sometimes has brownish markings. Females are brown with a yellow stripe on the body.

HABITS & HABITAT Very common and widespread across the region. Associated with water including wetlands, flowing streams and rivers as well as stagnant pools. Territorial males perch and defend areas near to them, chasing away other dragonflies and courting females.

Broad scarlet
Crocothemis erythraea

40–45mm Males are striking and easily recognised by their colouring. They have a vivid red body, abdomen and eyes and may seem to smoulder in the bright sunshine. Females are pale brown.

HABITS & HABITAT Common and widespread and may be found almost anywhere in East Africa, typically in wetlands and at water bodies lined with vegetation, especially sedges. Males chase each other and perch frequently on exposed stems, twigs or rocks. The broad abdomen distinguishes this species from the similar red-veined dropwing.

A. POWYS

Banded groundlings
Brachythemis spp.

25–30mm Very common and recognisable.
Males are among the most familiar insects, with
black bodies and unique dark brownish bands
on their wings. Females have yellow-and-black-
patterned bodies and clear wings.

HABITS & HABITAT Highly engaging, they tend
to follow people and animals in the grass around
wetlands. Gregarious and sometimes seen in
very large numbers, they enjoy perching on bare
ground close to water. Common from coastal to
highland areas, and around all Rift Valley lakes.

A POWYS

Barbet
Philonomon luminans

~40mm A stunningly beautiful and distinctive
dragonfly. Males have unique bright orange
and yellow colouring. The abdomen is boldly
marked with yellow and has an orange-red base.
Females are blackish, with yellow markings.

HABITS & HABITAT A widespread but not very
common species that favours quieter wetlands
as well as pools or ponds lined with vegetation
in savanna areas. Can be shy, but also returns to
favourite perches, making it a good subject for
photography. Males court females at the edges
of wetlands.

Globe skimmer
Pantala flavescens

~50mm A robust and brightly coloured dragonfly.
Males and females are similar in colour. The
body is brown and orange, the face is bright
yellow and the eyes are brick red or orange.

HABITS & HABITAT One of the most enigmatic
East African dragonflies; this species has been
found to migrate into the region from India, via
the Maldives and the Seychelles in the Indian
Ocean. Groups of dragonflies arrive with the
southeast monsoons, and spread across East
Africa seeking seasonal pans or pools in which
to breed. Gregarious, feeding and moving
in groups.

African black widow

Palpopleura lucia

~30mm A small but instantly recognisable dragonfly. Males are unique and distinctive, with black-marked or patterned wings and pale powder blue bodies. Females are dull yellow and black with similar, but duller, wing markings.
HABITS & HABITAT Common and widespread across East Africa, from coastal to inland and highland areas. Found among dense vegetation along the edges of streams and wetlands. Can be very common in some swamps and in drying pools of seasonal rivers. Tame and confiding; easy to approach.

Julia skimmer

Orthetrum julia

~55mm A noticeable dragonfly that has a pale blue body and robust build. In bright sunlight the males have striking marbled green eyes. Females are dull with blackish, olive green and yellow markings.
HABITS & HABITAT One of the most abundant, common and widespread dragonflies in highland forest, grassland and savanna habitats. Many males will patrol and scrap at the edges of streams. Often basks in the sunshine, perched on logs, rocks or stems.

Rock dweller

Bradinopyga cornuta

40–45mm A large but often overlooked dragonfly. Males and females are similarly patterned with pale yellow markings on a blackish-brown body. Superbly camouflaged (see arrow) when they rest on speckled or lichen-covered rocks.
HABITS & HABITAT These intriguing dragonflies are found along faster-flowing streams and rivers, especially in rocky gorges. They move swiftly and spend long periods of time perched on rocks basking in the sunshine. Can be approached if they don't notice that they are being watched; otherwise shy.

M N MUTISO

Gregarious cockroaches *Cartoblatta* spp.

20–25mm Gregarious. Nymphs are often found clustered together. Adults and nymphs have compact shiny bodies, covered with bright orange and yellow spots. The clusters of spots are often noticeable from some distance, which may serve as a warning to predators.

HABITS & HABITAT Found in bush, savanna, forest, woodland and coastal regions in East Africa. The nymphs are driven by pheromones to aggregate, and can secrete chemical defences if harassed.

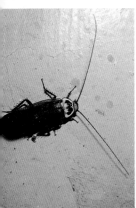

Common cockroaches *Periplaneta* spp.

25–35mm One of the most recognisable and familiar insects throughout the world. Adults have long legs that enable them to run swiftly. Their bodies are the familiar reddish-brown colour that everyone knows.

HABITS & HABITAT These insects are closely associated with humans. They have adapted to living in houses, especially in food stores and pantries. More active at night, they are often seen running when the lights are suddenly turned on. Can be a serious pest by fouling stored food and are implicated in transferring germs, due to their indiscriminate tastes.

Blattelid wood roaches BLATELLIDAE

10–15mm Compact and flat-bodied cockroaches that are typically dark blackish-brown, or brown with limited markings. Immature nymphs are wingless with clearly visible abdominal segments. Adults have wings.

HABITS & HABITAT Common and widespread in all habitats. Typically found when rocks, stones or decaying logs are lifted up and the roaches attempt to scurry to safety. A number of species live inside the nests of ants or termites. They feed on detritus scavenged in the hidden places where they live.

Snouted termites

Trinervitermes spp.

~5mm Small termites; workers and soldiers are similar in size. The heads of members of the soldier caste are a very distinctive oval shape and taper to form a specialised snout. The jaws of both workers and soldiers are not large.
HABITS & HABITAT Among the most interesting termites, they use their specialised 'snouts' to squirt a repellent sticky fluid as a unique means of chemical defence against ants. Typically shy, they forage among grasses at night, and are usually noticed when their compact nests are disturbed in grasslands.

Harvester termites

Hodotermes spp.

Workers 8–10mm, soldiers ~15mm Robust termites. The soldiers and workers have striped bodies and very dark brown heads that sometimes appear black in colour. The queen is enlarged and stays deep in her nest.
HABITS & HABITAT One of the most intriguing and specialised termites of African savannas. Most common in wetter grasslands in southern Kenya, extending into Tanzania and further west and south. Frantically active during the day, when workers emerge to cut grass that they chew and process inside their nests.

Fungus-growing termites

Macrotermes spp.

Workers ~5mm, soldiers ~15mm Workers are tiny, pale and blind with soft white bodies. Soldiers have massive hard heads with sickle-shaped jaws that terminate in sharp points. The queen is enormous, engorged and remains deep inside the mound.
HABITS & HABITAT One of the classic species of the African savanna and bush. In hot areas large mounds with 'chimneys' up to 6m are constructed (top image). Plant matter is chewed and digested using a fungus. These termites cultivate the fungi, just like humans cultivate crops, so this is a true form of agriculture. The termites form an important part of the nutrient cycle on the savannas and their mounds offer shelter to many other creatures.

Green mantids
Sphrodomantis spp.

40–50mm Large and striking mantids that are bright green, sometimes with pale yellow or white markings. Females more heavily built than males, often with swollen abdomens, and they have shorter wings. Eyes prominent with a distinctive fovea, which functions like a pupil, allowing the insect to fix its gaze.

HABITS & HABITAT Common and widespread throughout all major habitats, including bush, savanna, forest and riverine areas. Often enters buildings or lodges, drawn to the lights. Stalks and hunts insect prey on vegetation.

Flower mantids
HYMENOPODIDAE

40–45mm One of the most striking and unique insects found in the region. Nymphs are elaborate and covered with ornamented lobes, and colour varies from mottled green and cream to pink (as in the *Pseudocreobotra* pictured here). Adults are mottled pink and green, with an eyespot on each wing.

HABITS & HABITAT They move slowly and methodically and can often be found perched on flowering acacias, desert roses and other plants where they ruthlessly seize and feed on flower-visiting insects. Nymphs will curl their abdomens up when threatened.

Bark mantids
MANTIDAE

30–40mm Small to medium-sized praying mantids that are superbly camouflaged with mottled grey-brown colouring and a narrow build that helps them blend in perfectly with the background (inset shows dorsal view). Wings can be boldly patterned, but are usually folded away, so are rarely seen.

HABITS & HABITAT Very common, but often overlooked during the day as they are so well hidden. Often seen at night around lights where they sometimes catch and eat other insects drawn to the light. In some species females provide protection for their oothecae (egg cases) by standing guard over them.

Grass mantids

MANTIDAE

50–75mm Large, narrow-bodied mantids that are well camouflaged in grassland habitats. Typically pale brown, tan or beige, with flecks of darker colour. Wings brightly coloured and patterned, though only seen in flight.

HABITS & HABITAT Members of this group of mantids are usually encountered on grassland walks and occasionally around lights at night in grassland and savanna areas. Grass mantids can be shy and typically don't move when first encountered, relying on their camouflage to escape detection, and fleeing into grass if pursued.

A. POWYS

Leaf mantids

MANTIDAE

80–90mm Large, striking and very noticeable mantids. Robustly built, most of these mantids are various shades of green (occasionally brown) and have flecks or patches of lighter colour on the wings or body.

HABITS & HABITAT Bold and confident, these mantids are usually found perched on leafy bushes or flowering clumps of plants, where they ambush insects. Can be aggressive when challenged and will fix anyone who bothers them with the classic mantid stare, following their 'attacker's' movements carefully and lashing out with their forelegs if further harassed.

Cone-headed mantids

EMPUSIDAE

60–75mm Large, elegant mantids. Nymphs and adults have slender, elongated bodies. Colouring varies with species, but nymphs are typically mottled brown and grey, with flecks in paler colours, while adults can be green and cream, brown or tan, sometimes with colourful wings or patches.

HABITS & HABITAT One of the most charming of the mantids, the cone-headed mantids move confidently on vegetation and pause often to scan their surroundings. Found in moist habitats including woodlands, forest, riverine and coastal bush areas. Voracious predators, they will catch and kill almost anything.

Common earwigs
DERMAPTERA

5–10mm Small insects that have distinctive long, flattened bodies, with short wings that don't cover their backs, leaving most of the abdominal segments visible. Colouring brownish with red or orange, wings often dark. The pointed, curved, usually short forceps at the tip of the abdomen are a distinctive feature.

HABITS & HABITAT Furtive, shy and mostly nocturnal, earwigs are most often encountered when logs or rocks are moved or lifted. Sometimes seen running for shelter along the ground during the rains. Little is known about their biology, although they are mostly omnivorous and live in burrows.

Long-horned earwigs
DERMAPTERA

5–10mm Small to medium-sized insects that have distinctive long, flattened bodies, with short wings that do not cover the back and leave most of the abdominal segments visible. Generally brown or black. The long, pointed, curved forceps at the end of the abdomen are distinctive.

HABITS & HABITAT Furtive, shy and largely nocturnal, earwigs are most often encountered when logs or rocks are moved or lifted. If threatened, they will curve the abdomen over the back and snap at an attacker with their forceps, but are otherwise harmless.

Stoneflies
PLECOPTERA

5–25mm Small to medium-sized insects that are soft-bodied, large-eyed and have long, thin, tapering antennae. Nymphs are wingless, aquatic and have gills for breathing in water. Adults have wings that are folded flat on their backs. Generally brown or tan, sometimes patterned, and paler on the underside.

HABITS & HABITAT An ancient group of insects that live in association with cool, flowing, well-oxygenated streams in the highland areas of East Africa. Usually seen sunning themselves on rocks in or along streams, they move weakly and rarely fly.

E.M. GITONGA

Camel crickets RHAPHIDOPHORIDAE

10–60mm Nymph size varies depending on species and maturity. Adults in this group typically have very long legs and long, thin, tapering antennae. Bodies pale to dark brown, sometimes with reddish or tan hues.

HABITS & HABITAT A distinctive group of crickets. Often found in caves and other sheltered places, including hidden corners of thatched huts. Frequently encountered in small groups, they move slowly and feel their way around in the dark using their long antennae. They are omnivorous and scavenge on whatever they can.

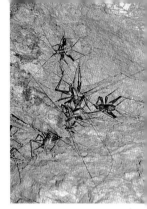

Armoured ground crickets BRADYPORINAE

20–50mm Size variable, but most East African species are medium to large insects. Have heavily built, stout bodies. Thorax and legs are armoured with spines and protuberances. Colour variable, from mottled green to brown.

HABITS & HABITAT Despite their formidable appearance, these are sluggish and harmless insects. They feed mainly on plants, but are known to be cannibalistic when the opportunity arises. Slow moving, can easily be picked up and closely observed. Will sometimes feign death if harassed or startled. Eaten by jackals, mongooses and bat-eared foxes.

Bush crickets TETTIGONIIDAE

55–65mm Size variable depending on maturity. Bodies robustly built and can be quite narrow, with wings folded down. In females the ovipositor, which is used for laying eggs in soil, is visible as a curved, knife-like tip to the abdomen.

HABITS & HABITAT Very common and widespread in bush, savanna and grassland habitats. Active during the day. Often found on flowering bushes where they browse on leaves, flowers and other plant parts. Some species are considered pests, especially on irrigated farms within dryland areas.

Common katydids
TETTIGONIIDAE

50–60mm Has the long hind legs and long antennae typical of a katydid. Wings are folded down over the back, giving the body a triangular profile. A bright uniform green, although some forms are pale brown.

HABITS & HABITAT One of East Africa's most familiar insects. Large numbers of adults are drawn to lights, especially at the beginning of the rains, and can be very obvious around city streetlights in Nairobi, Kampala and Dar es Salaam. Widely consumed in western regions, including in Uganda where a small-scale canning industry is based on these insects.

Leaf katydids
TETTIGONIIDAE

60–80mm Size varies; forest-dwelling species tend to be larger. Wings are wrapped over the robust body, giving a flat or cylindrical appearance, depending on the species. Has long, thin antennae. The long hind legs are held near the body at rest. May be various shades of green, sometimes with mottling that mimics leaf damage.

HABITS & HABITAT Members of this group are beautifully camouflaged and seem to disappear when resting against foliage. Often seen when startled into flight, and sometimes drawn to lights at night. They feed on plants; some species have specialised to feed on fig trees.

Bark katydids
TETTIGONIIDAE

55–65mm Size varies depending on maturity. Have compact bodies with long antennae. The wings are folded flat; they overlap and cover the back. May be shades of brown, grey, mottled red, mottled orange or mottled black.

HABITS & HABITAT Very common and widespread in bush, savanna and grassland habitats. Often drawn to lights and found resting on tent flaps or walls. Mostly nocturnal. Will flash colourful abdomen if alarmed. During the day found resting, superbly camouflaged (see arrow), in sheltered areas on tree trunks.

Common crickets
Gryllus spp.

20–25mm Medium-sized to large. Males are familiar, shiny black insects and fold their wings over their backs. Females tend to be duller, blackish-brown or reddish. Both sexes have spines protruding from the tip of the abdomen.
HABITS & HABITAT One of the most familiar and abundant of all insects. Widespread in gardens, towns and in association with people. Found in drains and corners of rooms and well known for chirping, which starts at dusk and continues into the night. Sound is produced by rubbing the wings together over stridulating ridges.

Mole crickets
GRYLLOTALPIDAE

20–35mm Small to medium-sized insects. Bodies hairy, cylindrical and very robust, perfectly designed for burrowing and moving through soil. Their most obvious feature is the pair of greatly enlarged and modified forelegs, used for digging. Rich sepia and pale brown in colour.
HABITS & HABITAT Found in moist areas and often seen at night when they move on the surface of the ground. Otherwise mostly subterranean, feeding on the roots of plants. Can be a pest in horticulture. Their meandering subsurface burrows are a common feature in wet soils. The male's call is a distinctive, continuous buzz.

C. GRIFFITHS & M. PICKER

Grouse/Pygmy Locusts
TETRIGIDAE

5–10mm Tiny insects that are typically uniformly coloured, ranging from shiny black to grey-brown. Often coated with mud and difficult to see. Adults of the common species have enlarged hind legs and long wings that project to a point.
HABITS & HABITAT Members of this common and widespread group are associated with the edges of water bodies, including lakes, swamps and slow-flowing rivers with mud flats. They live in burrows and feed on rich algal mats at the surface. Can be very abundant, rising in thousands when disturbed by animals walking along the mud flats.

CRICKETS, KATYDIDS, LOCUSTS & GRASSHOPPERS

Common garden locust

Acanthacris ruficornis

50–100mm Large insects with bold cream-striped bodies. The forewings and thorax are dark brown, the hind wings greenish-yellow and only seen in flight. Hind legs well-developed with spines.
HABITS & HABITAT Widespread and very common, including on farms and in gardens. Feed on a wide range of plants, including some vegetables and garden flowers. Large eggs are laid in soil. Flight noisy and often rather clumsy in adults. Can be handled, but known to kick; the spiny legs occasionally break human skin.

Milkweed locusts

Phymateus spp.

60–90mm Large insects that are easily noticed when perched on bushes. Adults are bright green with some red, blue and yellow markings. Wings are red and blue, shown in flight or when alarmed. Females are larger than males. Nymphs are boldly patterned and multicoloured and appear wingless, although the wings are just short and undeveloped.
HABITS & HABITAT A familiar insect of bush, grassland and savanna. Common on *Gomphocarpus* spp. and other milkweeds. Nymphs gather in gregarious clusters that often startle people. Females are larger and males are often found riding on their backs. Both sexes release defensive noxious chemicals if harassed.

Red desert locusts

Nomadacris spp.

50–75mm Large, long-bodied, elegant locusts. Wings are long and folded closely together at rest. Colouring varies, from pale brown to bright red-brown with black or dark brown mottling. Hind wings have red or purple markings, visible in flight.
HABITS & HABITAT One of the more infamous insects of the region. These species and the related migratory desert locusts sometimes form large swarms that travel and consume crops. Found in warmer dryland areas of northern Kenya and northern Uganda and drier regions of Tanzania.

Stick grasshoppers
Truxalis spp.

60–70mm Large insects with elegant, tapered bodies and narrow, elongated heads. Colour varies from pale brown to bright green, with clear, yellow or purple hind wings. The nymphs are even more slender and are often paler than the adults.

HABITS & HABITAT Very common and widespread in grasslands, bush and savanna across East Africa. They tend to favour areas with longer grass, where they can hide. They feed on grasses, including several tough species that other creatures can't digest, such as wire grass (*Pennisetum* spp.). Eggs are laid in damp, sandy soil.

Dryland grasshoppers
Sphingonotus spp.

~30mm Small to medium-sized grasshoppers. Compact and narrow with wings folded back and tapering to a point. Colour and pattern are highly variable and, generally, closely match the soil colour: from red-brown to a pale sandy colour. Hind wings are often a brighter colour or have markings that are visible only in flight.

HABITS & HABITAT One of the most widespread and familiar groups of grasshoppers in arid and semi-arid regions. They appear to favour bare, rocky or sandy ground. Can survive in some very arid regions of northern Kenya and Uganda and into the Horn of Africa. An important component of dryland ecology both as herbivores and as a source of food for many birds and mammals. Make short 'hopping' flights.

Field grasshoppers
ACRIDIDAE

20–30mm Size and colouring vary depending on the species, the weather and the condition of the vegetation. Typically brown with darker patches or markings (*Oedalus* spp.). They have compact bodies. Legs are folded when at rest. Males slightly smaller than females.

HABITS & HABITAT A very diverse, widespread and familiar group of 'typical' grasshoppers. They feed on a wide range of short grasses and can be voracious seasonally, consuming large amounts of forage. Males are often found in association with females, riding on their backs.

Giant stick insects   *Bactrododema* spp.

100–250mm One of the longest insects in the region (inset shows scale); females are more than double the length of the males. They are dark brown to grey, with some very fine mottling. The hind wings, normally tucked away from view, are blackish and beautifully patterned with lighter spots. The related 'walking stick' (*Palophus reyi*) is the longest insect in the world: its length outstretched is >40cm.

HABITS & HABITAT Moves with a slow, swaying gait, and seems to gently feel its way along with its legs. Males and females are often found together – the male clinging to the female. Attracted to lights, and often found in the morning on walls or the sides of tents in warmer bush and savanna areas.

Grass stick insects   BACILLIDAE

50–100mm Medium-sized and very slender insects. Males tend to be brown or pale and are often wingless. Females are larger, various shades of green or brown and green, with stripes for camouflage.

HABITS & HABITAT Common and widespread, but often overlooked as they are so well hidden. Move slowly, twitching slightly as if part of a plant swayed by the breeze. Males spend long periods in copulation with females. Herbivorous and feed primarily on grasses. Found in grassland and savanna, including highland areas.

Leaf stick insects   PHASMIDA

60–110mm Large insects; the females are about twice as large as males. Colour highly variable, ranging from mottled brown to greenish, with tinges of other colours. Body appears slightly rough, which aids in camouflage.

HABITS & HABITAT Uncommon inhabitants of forest, especially where trees are covered in moss and epiphytes. Often overlooked as they are absolute masters of camouflage. They feed and move about slowly on tree trunks and among the leaves of ferns and orchids. Found in warmer forest habitats in western regions.

M N MUTISO

Bark lice

PSOCOPTERA

1–2mm Tiny, soft-bodied insects with large eyes. Their wings are delicate, frequently with a marbled pattern, although some species are wingless. Often cryptic and easily overlooked. They vary from pale to brown to mottled black.
HABITS & HABITAT A widespread and ubiquitous, yet rarely noticed, group of insects. Can be found in a wide range of habitats including on bark, sheltered parts of trees, under rocks and even in houses. They feed on plants, lichens, fungi and detritus. The related domestic book lice are pests of stored products, especially paper.

Human lice

PEDICULIDAE

1–2mm Tiny insects that have pale bodies and an oval, elongate appearance. The 'nits' are the most obvious life stage – when observed closely they look like whitish flecks attached to individual strands of human head hair.
HABITS & HABITAT Common and widespread. Easily move between people sharing a space or in close contact. Often spread through sharing of combs or hairbrushes. Human body (pubic) lice are related, but not as common. Control is typically achieved with improved sanitation, fumigation of bedding and houses, and individual treatment of infestations.

M. PICKER & C. GRIFFITHS

Bird lice

PHILOPTERIDAE

2–10mm Small to medium-sized insects. Robust, with strong grappling legs for holding on to feathers. Shape, colour and size vary depending on the species, but they are often pale or brownish in colour.
HABITS & HABITAT Common and widespread parasites of virtually all bird species. Highly host-specific, individual bird lice will often be found on just one species of bird. They feed on the soft, downy feathers, and have specialised digestive systems capable of handling this diet. They remain on their hosts for their entire lives; never found free-living.

M. PICKER & C. GRIFFITHS

M. PICKER & C. GRIFFITHS

Bed bugs

CIMICIDAE

~3mm Tiny insects that have compressed, flattened, oval-shaped bodies and a large, rounded abdomen that can engorge as they feed. The mouthparts form a piercing tube that is ideal for puncturing the skin of mammals and birds.
HABITS & HABITAT Common, widespread and ubiquitous in association with human dwellings and bedding (in the case of one cosmopolitan species), with the bulk of diversity occurring on bats in their roosts. They adopt a bizarre reproductive strategy called 'traumatic insemination' whereby males inseminate females by rupturing their body walls.

Plant bugs

MIRIDAE

2–10mm A variable and diverse group of mostly small insects. Compact, rounded bodies with variable colouring. Most species are green, red, brown or shiny black, sometimes with lighter areas. Most species have wings.
HABITS & HABITAT An economically important group, as these diverse bugs will feed on almost any plant, piercing it and sucking out its juices. A few species are scavengers or predators of aphids and other plant-feeding insects.

Lace bugs

TINGIDAE

4–5mm One of the most distinctive groups in the order known as Hemiptera or true bugs. Generally small or medium in size. Lace bugs are named for the distinctive, elegant sculpturing on their wings and bodies. Colour variable – cream, green or brown. The body is often patterned.
HABITS & HABITAT A diverse and variable group, whose members are exclusively plant-feeders. Shy and retiring, lace bugs will typically feed while hidden, often on the underside of a leaf. Can cause yellowing on foliage as well as leaf drop in some crops.

M. PICKER

Assassin bugs REDUVIIDAE

10–15mm A widespread group of predatory insects. Robustly built with a compact, slightly hourglass shape. They have powerful legs and bulging eyes. The mouthparts form a curved, dagger-like beak used for stabbing prey.
HABITS & HABITAT Voracious predators that stalk, ambush and kill all kinds of insect prey whenever they can. Prey are immobilised by injecting venom that paralyses them and allows the assassin bug to feed by sucking out the liquid insides. Often attracted to lights at night. May bite if handled.

Ant-cloaking assassin bugs REDUVIIDAE

5–15mm One of the most remarkable insects of East Africa: the distinctive nymphs cloak themselves with the bodies of dead prey that have been sucked dry. Their size varies depending on species and the maturity of the nymph. Adults are shiny, flat-bodied and often have bright spots or markings.
HABITS & HABITAT An enigmatic insect. Nymphs can be found in small groups among the buttress roots of figs and other forest trees in more tropical areas. They move slowly and methodically, waiting along ant trails to grab their victims. Adults are sometimes found in the vicinity of the nymphs.

Giant assassin bugs *Platymeris* spp.

45–55mm A large and striking assassin bug. Body very robust, with an elegant outline and strong, flat wings. Black with bright orange, yellow or whitish spots: considered a classic example of warning coloration. Mouthparts form a sharp beak.
HABITS & HABITAT Fairly common and widespread, especially in warmer bush and savanna habitats. Often drawn to camp lights at night, where it will stalk and kill other insects. Can deliver a very painful bite and should not be handled or provoked.

Water measurers
HYDROMETRIDAE

10–15mm Medium-sized insects with a very narrow build: body is almost thread-like, with long, very spindly legs. Has piercing mouthparts used for holding prey, and long, jointed antennae.
HABITS & HABITAT Quite common at the edges of relatively still waters in ponds, sheltered pools and wetlands. They move slowly and methodically, balancing on the surface of the water using their specialised legs. They scavenge for, or seize, prey, often holding it in their mouth for long periods.

Twig wilters
COREIDAE

10–15mm A widespread and distinctive group of true bugs. Medium-sized with a stout build and typically dull black bodies. Mouthparts are adapted for piercing plants and sucking out their juices. Hind legs often enlarged, appearing muscular.
HABITS & HABITAT Many species are specialised to feed on specific plants, including cycads and members of the squash family. They feed by piercing young shoots and injecting saliva to aid feeding, which ultimately destroys the growing shoots. Found in fairly moist areas including forest, woodland and gardens.

Leaf-footed bugs
COREIDAE

10–20mm A group of true bugs that is distinguished by modified hind legs, which have large, flap-like protuberances. Colour varies depending on the species, but some can be very colourful with beige, orange or red markings or spots on a black background.
HABITS & HABITAT Common and widespread in bush, savanna and woodland regions. Some species are pests of cultivated crops, including passion fruits, oranges, lemons, pumpkins and watermelons. Often found feeding on the fruit of wild shrubs including *Turraea*. They vibrate their antennae when alarmed or approached.

Cotton stainer nymphs PYRRHOCORIDAE

5–15mm Familiar and widespread. Body red with black markings. They form distinctive clusters of bright red-and-black insects of varying sizes. Their mouthparts are piercing tubes for feeding on plants.

HABITS & HABITAT The nymphs are often mistaken for a different species (see below). These plant-feeders are regarded as pests in some areas. Their bright colours serve as a warning signal and they aggregate in groups, which enhances this effect.

M.N. MUTISO

Cotton stainers *Dysdercus spp.*

~15mm Among the most recognisable East African insects. Named for the damage they do when feeding on buds, although they do also soil cotton bolls. These are the adults of the nymphs described above. Boldly marked in beige or tan and black, sometimes with red or orange markings. Females slightly larger than males. Mouthparts form a tube for piercing plants.

HABITS & HABITAT Widely distributed in most habitats, including gardens and farms. Adults sometimes found in the vicinity or company of the nymphs, but also commonly encountered alone. Can be pests of okra (ladies' fingers) and a serious pest of cotton in some areas. Pairs often found in copulation (as pictured here).

M.N. MUTISO

Seed bugs LYGAEIDAE

10–15mm A group of medium-sized true bugs. Quite elegant and pretty insects with slender or rounded bodies, long segmented antennae and compact heads. Both nymphs and adults can be colourful, often with bright orange or red patterns.

HABITS & HABITAT Mostly herbivorous insects that feed on seeds, which they pierce using their mouthparts. Some species are specialised and can reliably be found on particular plants, such as the milkweed bug (pictured here), found on milkweed. Common in a wide range of habitats, including gardens and cultivated areas.

Picasso bugs
Sphaerocoris spp.

~10mm Among the most striking of all true bugs, these are medium-sized insects with a compact, oval shape. Distinctive bold patterning in blue-green, orange, red and black on a pale ivory background. Nymphs are rounder, pale orange and black.

HABITS & HABITAT Abundant and widespread in grassland, savanna and moist habitats, especially after the start of the rains, when they can be found in small groups feeding on plants. They feed on a wide range of plants including both shrubs and herbs and are sometimes found on garden plants.

Rainbow shield bugs
Calidea spp.

10–15mm Has a slightly elongated body that tapers somewhat towards the abdomen. Colouring is unique and unmistakable: a blue-green background, with blue spots and yellow markings, and red sides. Body robust, metallic and shiny.

HABITS & HABITAT Common and widespread in a wide range of habitats across the region, from woodlands to bush to more arid areas. Occurs on many different plants including cultivated crops, tobacco, castor oil, garden plants and even highly toxic succulents and *Jatropha* (Euphorbiaceae).

Pill bugs
PLATASPIDAE

5–20mm Uniquely shaped, rather squat, rounded bugs that are dull black and covered with fine spots or speckling in white, orange or yellow. The rounded back is actually the thorax, which is expanded to enclose the insect's body. Nymphs are whitish.

HABITS & HABITAT Widespread in fairly moist woodland, savanna and tropical forest areas. Nymphs live in aggregations closely clustered together. Often found on wild legumes where they sit still feeding, but on the whole the biology of these insects is poorly known.

M N MUTISO

Shield-backed bugs SCUTELLERIDAE

5–10mm A striking group of true bugs whose
members are very similar to beetles and are
often mistaken for ladybird beetles. Body
rounded and squat, with a convex profile when
viewed from the side. Colour varies. Nymphs
are often brightly coloured.
HABITS & HABITAT Common and widespread
in bush, savanna and woodland habitats. They
feed on plants using their piercing and sucking
mouthparts. Immature nymphs of some species
are gregarious and found in groups, sometimes
with the mother in attendance. Found primarily
on members of the hibiscus family (Malvaceae).

A. POWYS

Green stink bugs PENTATOMIDAE

~10mm A highly diverse and variable group of
insects, members of which have a distinctive
'shield' shape and a large triangular section on
the middle of the back. Green stink bugs include
several different species, all with uniform
green bodies. Wings sometimes have a darker
patch, as in the common green vegetable
bugs (*Nezara* spp.).
HABITS & HABITAT Common, ubiquitous and
widespread insects. Found on hundreds of
different plant species, including many crops,
where they can be pests. They feed on various
tender plant parts, and the wounds inflicted by
their mouthparts eventually cause damage.

Spotted stink bugs PENTATOMIDAE

~10mm A widespread group of boldly marked,
striking insects. They have the classic triangular
stink bug shape, often with short spines on
the sides of the thorax. Most species are tan,
brown or darker, with pale spots or patches.
HABITS & HABITAT Common and widespread
in moist grassland, savanna, woodland and
forest-edge areas. Often associated with
herbaceous vegetation, where they can be
found perched on flowering spikes during the
day. They move slowly, flicking their antennae,
and often drop to the ground if harassed.

Sunflower seed bugs PENTATOMIDAE

~10mm A widespread and recognisable group of bugs, members of which have a narrow head with a broader body and mottled, red-brown wings folded neatly over the back, but revealing the edges of the abdomen, which is banded in yellow or orange and black.

HABITS & HABITAT Common and ubiquitous across the region. Found in a wide range of habitat types, especially where sunflowers are cultivated, where they can be a pest. Also found on a number of plants, mostly wildflowers, including flowering *Leucas* and *Leonotis* spp., especially in years of good rains.

E.M. GITONGA

Antestia bugs *Antestia* spp.

5–10mm Members of this group are highly variable. Typically shiny black with various markings, including spots, speckles and patches of colour (orange, green, white or yellow).

HABITS & HABITAT A common and widespread group especially familiar to farmers and gardeners in East Africa. They feed on a wide range of plants, including many cultivated crops. Important pests of coffee, citrus and other fruit trees, which they damage by feeding on shoots, causing wilting.

Large leafhoppers CIXIIDAE

10–25mm Members of this insect group are diverse and variable. Wings are rather broad and somewhat rounded, held flatter over the body than is seen in most other similar bugs (such as planthoppers and other groups of leafhoppers). Colour varies depending on the species.

HABITS & HABITAT These striking insects are typically found perched on their host plants in moist riverine bush, woodland and forest areas. Can be found in small groups or singly. They use their mouthparts to pierce plant stems and suck out the juices.

Broad-headed bugs ALYDIDAE

15–20mm Medium-sized insects with distinctive triangular, fairly wide heads (relative to their bodies) that are rounded in front and have bulging eyes. Colour varies depending on the species – may be black, red, orange or brownish.
HABITS & HABITAT These seed-feeding bugs can be seasonally common around the plants that they exploit. They move swiftly and are active, mobile insects. They feed on seeds using their piercing mouthparts. Rather nervous and twitchy, they will fly away if bothered.

Water striders GERRIDAE

5–20mm Also known as pond skaters or 'Jesus bugs'. Common and familiar insects with narrow, streamlined bodies and long, well-developed legs that propel them across the surface of water. Black or dark with some pale patches.
HABITS & HABITAT Distinctive insects that move swiftly on the surfaces of ponds, puddles and slow-flowing streams. Opportunistic predators and scavengers, they feed on insects that fall onto the surface of the water. They glide nimbly thanks to specialised hairs on their feet that repel water and don't break the surface tension.

Backswimmers NOTONECTIDAE

5–10mm Typically small insects with a slender, extremely streamlined build and distinctive elongated, powerful hind legs used to swim with a rowing motion. They are brown, tan or blackish, with or without spots or patches.
HABITS & HABITAT Powerful swimmers found in calm or stagnant water, often in large numbers. These predators catch and subdue prey in the water, ranging from insects to tadpoles and, rarely, small fish. They surface periodically to breathe air directly, and flee if disturbed. Can also fly. Sometimes drawn to lights.

Giant water bugs BELOSTOMATIDAE

20–100mm Among the most noticeable of the true bugs. The largest species are heavily built, powerful insects. Forelegs are well developed and have sharp, hooked ends. They are streamlined and perfectly adapted for swimming.

HABITS & HABITAT Seasonally fairly common in the vicinity of water bodies. Most often seen when flying noisily into lights in camps or houses, where they often fall down and move about in confusion. Voracious predators, they have been recorded eating fish, tadpoles and even small birds!

M.N. MUTISO

Brooding water bugs *Appassus* spp.

15–20mm Medium-sized insects with streamlined, flattened bodies and light brown, tan or grey-brown colouring. Males are easily identified when carrying a clutch of eggs.

HABITS & HABITAT An interesting example of paternal care: males carry around the eggs, which are glued to their backs. They favour clean waters with plenty of aquatic vegetation, through which they can usually be found crawling. Active predators, they feed on aquatic insects, small tadpoles and young or tiny fish.

C. GRIFFITHS & M. PICKER

Water scorpions NEPIDAE

20–75mm Large, striking insects that have well-built, narrow, streamlined bodies. Their front legs are well developed and are modified with hooked tips that enable them to grasp prey. Their distinctive feature is a long, narrow 'tail', or siphon, that serves as a breathing tube (hence the name 'scorpion').

HABITS & HABITAT Fairly common in ponds, pools and still water bodies with vegetation. Can usually be found partially hidden in the vegetation, using their siphons to breathe air. These predators feed on many different aquatic creatures.

Flatid bug nymphs

FLATIDAE

~10mm A unique group of insects in which nymphs look very different from adults: their bodies are generally pale – whitish, light green, cream or ivory – and covered in powdery wax. The most distinctive feature of these nymphs is a curly, untidy, brush-like tail made of wax.

HABITS & HABITAT Gregarious, typically found in small groups. Slow-moving and somewhat nervous. Will freeze at first if bothered, then either drop down or move away. They feed on plants using their piercing mouthparts. Occur in warm areas of forest, moist bush and woodland.

Flatid bug adults

FLATIDAE

10–25mm Beautiful winged insects that often sit in clusters. Colour highly variable, even within a single group. They vary from green to yellow or orange and many shades in between. Wings are held close to the body, folded downward, giving a distinctive triangular outline.

HABITS & HABITAT Adult flatid bugs are also known as flower bugs. When clustered, they are thought to resemble flowering spikes. They generally stay relatively still, but hop or fly away weakly when disturbed. Found in forest and woodland habitats.

Spittle bugs

CERCOPIDAE

~10mm Rarely seen, as each spittle bug is encased inside a foamy mass, hence the common name. Spittle bugs are immature froghoppers (see next insect). They have narrow, pale greenish-white or yellowish bodies.

HABITS & HABITAT Immature nymphs, they inhabit a bubble of frothy spittle that they make by mixing plant sap, derived through feeding, with air. This is thought to help protect them from potential predators and parasites. They are passive when the 'spittle' is disturbed and can usually be found within, if the bubbles are gently parted.

Froghoppers
CERCOPIDAE

10–25mm A highly variable, striking group of insects. The adults are known as froghoppers, the immature nymphs as spittle bugs. Adults are brightly coloured in bold red, orange and shiny black. They have compact bodies, with wings held close and folded down.

HABITS & HABITAT These distinctive insects are the adult form of spittle bugs (see previous description). They sit on the leaves and stems of grasses and other plants, where they feed quietly, rarely moving. If disturbed, will hop away or fly very weakly. Found on lush grassy verges, on the edges of wetlands, on forest paths and in plantations.

Rain tree bug nymphs
Ptyelus spp.

10–15mm Immature rain tree bugs (described below) are often mistaken for another species. They are squat, oval-shaped, soft-bodied insects. Their bodies are typically yellow or whitish with black spots or stripes.

HABITS & HABITAT Highly gregarious. The name 'rain tree bugs' refers to the near-constant dripping of excreted fluid onto the ground (and any people below!) when they feed in the canopies of large trees. Often the nymphs are not noticed, apart from their dripping, as they don't move about and can be high up.

Rain tree bug adults
Ptyelus spp.

15–25mm Rain tree bug nymphs (described above) mature into reproductive adult rain tree bugs. They are boldly marked, striking insects that are typically bright yellow, grey or black, with variable patches and markings. Wings are long, smooth, and are folded down over the back. They have bright, shiny eyes.

HABITS & HABITAT Adults are mobile, fly weakly or land on the ground below the tree canopy and are often noticed. Typically found on leguminous trees including *Albizia* spp., acacias and introduced *Tipuana tipu*.

Giant forest cicadas CICADIDAE

60–90mm Large insects, whose wingspan can attain about 90mm. Stout and robust, having beautiful, transparent, strongly veined wings with green markings. Body colour varies from mottled green to mottled brown, with bright black eyes.

HABITS & HABITAT Noisy, shrill, almost deafening calls are a near-constant feature of the warmer and wetter forest and woodland regions of East Africa during the middle of the day. Males produce the sound using specialised tymbals and their hollow abdomens as resonators. Their biology is poorly known.

M.N. MUTISO

Green-winged cicadas *Stagira* spp.

30–40mm A very common groups of cicadas; its members have robustly built, but elegant, bodies and fine, clear wings with pale green veins. Bodies mostly plain apple green, but the actual shade varies. Eyes are often a contrasting colour (tan, orange or brownish).

HABITS & HABITAT Very common and widespread, including in gardens with mature trees. Most often noticed when nymphs emerge from the ground, climbing up, and leaving their cases on, tree trunks or walls. Immature nymphs feed on the roots of various plants, sometimes taking many years to develop. Adults feed on plant sap.

Brown cicadas CIDADIDAE

~30mm A group of common, small to medium-sized cicadas. Wings are transparent, tinged with pale colour, and have dark veins. Body is rich tan to ochre-yellow, with bright, contrasting eyes.

HABITS & HABITAT Very common and widespread in grassland, bush and more open savanna regions. Often emerge in large numbers after a few weeks of rain. Can be found clinging to the stems of grasses and herbs and are often noticed on walks through the bush.

Treehoppers
MEMBRACIDAE

5–10mm Stout, squat-bodied, heavily built insects. Wings are held over the body, which is often rounded and smooth, with a protruding point in the middle of the back (thorax). Colour varies – often cryptic, blending into the environment.

HABITS & HABITAT Common and widespread in bush, savanna, woodland and grassland habitats. Typically occur on trees and shrubs in forest and woodland understorey. Can be found singly as well as in small groups: immature nymphs tend to be more gregarious.

Thornbugs (ant-tended treehoppers)
MEMBRACIDAE

10–20mm Robust, rounded, wedge-shaped treehoppers. On the back of the thorax they have pronounced 'thorns', which can be exceedingly realistic and help these insects to blend in with plant stems.

HABITS & HABITAT As the alternative common name 'ant-tended treehoppers' suggests, these insects are most often found being tended by ants in warmer regions. They are common along the coastal zones of Kenya and Tanzania, where they are tended by weaver ants. Typically found on legumes and related species, and tend to favour acacias.

Leafhoppers
CICADELLIDAE

~10mm Common and ubiquitous insects. A highly variable group, members of which have a recognisable rounded, tubular shape, are typically small, and range in colour from green to shades of brown or yellow, often with flecks or stripes of a brighter hue.

HABITS & HABITAT A ubiquitous and abundant group of plant-feeding insects. People walking through herbs and grasses often notice them, as they jump readily when disturbed. Some are pests and can transmit viruses between plants. Mostly found in grassland habitats, or areas with lush grasses.

Whiteflies ALEYRODIDAE

2–3mm Tiny white insects most often noticed covering the undersides of leaves, including those of crop plants. Immature nymphs are blob-like lumps that don't move around. Adults are flimsy, winged insects, with rounded white wings.

HABITS & HABITAT Gregarious and ubiquitous, these insects are among the most important horticultural pests in the region. Different species occur in greenhouses and on citrus plants. They transmit viruses, secrete honeydew that attracts ants, and show signs of becoming resistant to pesticides in some areas.

Green aphids APHIDIDAE

1–2mm Common and familiar insects. Immature nymphs are tiny, round-bodied insects that cluster together. Adult females are large, and may be winged or wingless. It is the females that are typically encountered – males are only occasionally produced.

HABITS & HABITAT Common, ubiquitous and widespread insects that are most familiar as pests of garden plants and crops (see arrows). They have complex life cycles, sometimes involving more than one host plant, and in some species are able to reproduce asexually, with females giving birth to live young. They secrete honeydew and are tended by ants.

Milkweed aphids APHIDIDAE

1–2mm Common and widespread. Both nymphs and adults are often bright ochre-yellow, with black legs and eyes and black tubercles on their backs. Bodies fat, soft and rounded. Nymphs and adults are found in clusters that look like a growth on the plants. Winged forms are also produced, although most seem to be wingless, even as adults.

HABITS & HABITAT Common wherever milkweeds and their relatives grow (Asclepiadaceae). They feed in gregarious clusters where ants often tend them, and they fall victim to the larvae of ladybird beetles and lacewings.

Wax scale insects COCCIDAE

~10mm Lumpy, irregularly shaped, medium-sized insects. Body appears to be an indistinct blob, like molten wax, and feels waxy and soft. Typically white or whitish, with pinkish, brown or red streaks or marks.

HABITS & HABITAT Completely immobile as adults, although nymphs can move. Nymphs live on leaves and have a fringe of white scales or clumps of wax around them. Adults feed on plants. Female body greatly simplified, consisting of mouthparts, a stomach and an ovary. Males are winged, disperse from clusters to find females and are not often seen. Pests of gardens and crops.

♂

♀

Free-living scales COCCIDAE

5–10mm Small, variable and widespread insects. Females are blob-like, often pale orange or yellow, with distinct mouthparts for feeding and greatly reduced legs. Males are striking bright red or red-brown winged insects. Some males have long white tail streamers, the function of which is unclear.

HABITS & HABITAT Common insects that are often noticed in drylands at the beginning of the rains, when males can be seen flying low over the ground searching for females, which live underground, but surface briefly to mate.

Cochineal scale insects DACTYLOPIIDAE

5–10mm Familiar, if often overlooked insects. Both nymphs and adults are small, very soft insects that congregate in groups. Covered with loose, untidy, whitish wax that forms short filaments and easily rubs off.

HABITS & HABITAT Found exclusively on members of the cactus family, with which they have been either deliberately or accidentally introduced to East Africa. One species (*Dactylopius opuntiae*) is famous as the source of carmine, a deep red dye that was widely used and traded globally before synthetic dyes were developed.

M.N. MUTISO

Cottony cushion scales

Icerya spp.

5–10mm Familiar and widespread insects. Most obvious when clustered on plants, with distinctive, fluted white egg cases attached to their speckled red-brown or greyish bodies. Can occur in very dense clusters.

HABITS & HABITAT Very widespread, common and serious pests introduced from Australia. They have a bizarre but successful reproductive strategy: the population consists mainly of females that can also be hermaphrodites and self-fertilise. There are also some normal winged males that fertilise adult females. Found on many different plants, especially acacias.

Giant soft scales

MARGARODIDAE

15–30mm Females are large, noticeable lumps on garden trees and shrubs. Bodies oval, convex and bulging. Dark brown, but often appear pale because of their whitish wax covering. Attached to host trees by their undersides. Nymphs are flatter and wrinkled.

HABITS & HABITAT Common and widespread in moist habitats or seasonally in dry areas, where they can sometimes occur in large numbers on trees and shrubs. They secrete honeydew that attracts ants, and that accumulates and becomes mouldy near the feeding clusters. Found on many different trees and shrubs, including acacias, hibiscus and casuarinas.

E.M. GITONGA

Mealybugs

PSEUDOCOCCIDAE

2–4mm Tiny, often overlooked insects. Small greyish-white, oval bodies, edged with short, waxy filaments. There are many species, which are somewhat variable, but their overall shape and size are similar.

HABITS & HABITAT Widespread, common and ubiquitous plant-feeding insects. Found on a wide range of species, including many crops and garden plants. Some species are serious pests of citrus, grapevines, pears, apples, sugar cane and pineapples. Often attended and guarded by ants, which feed on the honeydew that they secrete.

Thrips
THYSANOPTERA

2–4mm Very tiny, slender insects that are common and widespread. Some species have wings. Colour varies – may be black, dark brown, banded or pale brown.

HABITS & HABITAT Ubiquitous and abundant insects that typically live and feed on plants. Most often noticed on flowers, where they are sometimes found in large numbers. Can be a pest in greenhouses and transmit viral diseases between plants. Capable of both sexual and asexual reproduction.

Brown lacewings
HEMEROBIIDAE

5–15mm Small, mostly dull brown or tan, with brownish markings on the wings. They have long antennae. The wings are folded down over the body when at rest.

HABITS & HABITAT Common and widespread in a wide range of habitats: grassland, bush, savanna, woodland, forests and gardens. Larvae are slug-like and of economic importance as they feed voraciously on aphids, hence are known as 'aphid wolves'. Adults are often attracted to lights in the rainy season and may be found resting on walls.

Green lacewings
CHRYSOPIDAE

15–50mm Elegant, beautiful, pale green insects. The wings are transparent, with exquisite fine green veins. Size varies, depending on species. Adults appear delicate, and the narrow abdomen is visible through the folded wings at rest.

HABITS & HABITAT Common and widespread in most habitats, including in drylands during the rains. They are attracted to lights and are often found perched on walls or tents. The larvae are very important predators of mealybugs and other pests. Widely used as a form of biological control in greenhouses and horticulture.

Antlion nymphs MYRMELEONTIDAE

10–20mm Large-jawed and round-bodied. Their sickle-shaped jaws inject venom into prey. Body appears rough, usually brown or grey-brown.

HABITS & HABITAT Well known in East Africa for the funnel-shaped pits they construct in sheltered spots (inset). However, most people have never seen the insects themselves. The pits are traps into which hapless insects (mainly ants) fall, sliding down into the antlion's waiting jaws.

Antlion adults MYRMELEONTIDAE

40–80mm The name 'antlion' is usually applied to the nymphs, as there is no widely accepted English common name for the adults. The wingspan of the adults varies with species. These are weak, flimsy, but elegant insects with clear wings (tinted or faintly spotted in some species). The body is long, the antennae are prominent and the wings are folded down over the body at rest.

HABITS & HABITAT Most often seen in the mornings or evenings on walks through grassland, as they fly up weakly when disturbed, then settle a short distance away, hanging vertically from grass stems. Drawn to lights and will often land on walls, tents and in camps. Adults are short-lived, as their sole purpose is reproduction.

Giant antlions *Palpares* spp.

~100mm Large, striking and elegant insects. The wings are clear, but heavily patterned with dark spots and patches. They have lean, but robust bodies, a hairy thorax and their antennae are curved and thickened at the ends.

HABITS & HABITAT Not uncommon insects of arid and semi-arid coastal bush, grassland and savanna regions. Often noticed when they fly into buildings or are found resting on walls. Occasionally flushed when walking – flight is clumsy and flapping. Larvae are free-living, opportunistic predators that dwell in sandy soil.

Black ground beetles   CARABIDAE

10–15mm Small to medium-sized insects. The abdomen is covered by the elytra (wing cases), giving an oval shape. They may have grooves or whitish hairs that resemble fine stripes. Head and thorax are robust. They have large, prominent eyes and long antennae.

HABITS & HABITAT A common and widespread group of insects in bush, grassland, savanna and forest glade areas where there are bare soils. Active both during the day and at night, and can often be found digging on sunny mornings during the rainy season. Voracious predators, they will feed on any insect that they can catch and subdue.

Striped velvet ground beetles

Graphipterus spp.

10–15mm Small to medium-sized insects. Robust, well built, with long legs and prominent head, bulging eyes and relatively large jaws. Body is shiny black or blackish with stripes of cream, yellow or tan depending on the species.

HABITS & HABITAT Active, alert and fast-moving beetles that run over the surface of the ground. Common in arid drylands, bush and savanna regions especially after rains. They move over the ground hunting other insects. More active during the day and often encountered along the edges of trails.

Ant-mimicking ground beetles

CARABIDAE

10–15mm Active, shiny black beetles. They have narrow, elegant bodies with a distinctive 'waist' that lends them an ant-like appearance. The rounded abdomen is sometimes marked with white spots, similar to those of female velvet ants (Mutillidae); other species have dull spots or none, more like the singing ants (*Pachycondyla* spp.).

HABITS & HABITAT They are active, mostly diurnal and move furtively and quickly, very like the velvet ants or large singing ants that they mimic. Predatory, feeding on many small insects and arthropods.

Spotted ground beetles CARABIDAE

40–60mm Striking, medium to large insects. Body is robust and athletic, with large eyes, large, powerful mandibles and long legs. The abdomen is often marked with spots (white, yellow or orange) and stripes.

HABITS & HABITAT Active, fast-moving, confident insects that move swiftly on the ground. Active mainly at dusk and at night, and often drawn to lights. Many species spray noxious chemical defences when bothered. They prey on a wide range of insects and other arthropods.

M N MUTISO

Burrowing ground beetles PASSALINAE

30–50mm A widespread group of ground beetles. They are uniformly coloured, usually blackish-brown or red, with thin, parallel veins in the wing cases, and straight-sided bodies. They have a thicker, heavier-set build than most ground beetles and massive, strong jaws.

HABITS & HABITAT Generally shy and slow-moving ground beetles, which are found when logs are overturned or when they occasionally fly into lights at night. They occur in a wide range of habitats, from arid regions to rainforests. They are strong insects that can easily dig into logs and the soil.

Marsh ground beetles *Bradybaenus* spp.

15–20mm Small to medium-sized beetles. They are tan with various green or darker markings and have a metallic sheen to their wings. The eyes and jaws are very prominent, as is typical of most predatory ground beetles.

HABITS & HABITAT Rather shy, but fairly common beetles found in sandy banks, wet mud flats and other such habitats in warm savanna, woodland and bush. They spend their day in burrows, emerging onto the mud or sand at night to hunt and feed on insects and other creatures.

Tiger beetle larvae
CICINDELINAE

15–25mm Fearsome-looking, large-headed and massive-jawed insects. The elongate body has a rough appearance. The large head is adapted for blocking the entrance to the burrows in which they live. Their middle body segments have hooks that help anchor them.

HABITS & HABITAT Found in a wide range of sandy and mud flat habitats at the edges of Rift Valley lakes, meandering rivers in drylands and other similar habitats. Generally found in warm low-altitude areas. Tiger beetle larvae excavate and live in burrows from which they ambush prey and emerge at night to hunt.

Spotted tiger beetles
CICINDELINAE

20–30mm Medium-sized beetles with an elegant, poised gait. Long legs and large, bulging eyes are distinctive features. Many different species occur, but spotted tiger beetles are often dark metallic green, purplish or blackish, with variable pale spots.

HABITS & HABITAT Found in the vicinity of streams, seasonal pools and other water bodies in warm, low-altitude areas of East Africa. Voracious predators that actively hunt around the edges of the water. They move swiftly and can both run and fly when approached. Often gregarious, and may be found in large numbers in suitable habitats.

Leopard tiger beetles
CICINDELINAE

10–20mm Small to medium-sized tiger beetles. They have attractive, shiny, copper-coloured bodies with variable patterns. Some species are more grey or brown. They have large, prominent eyes, long antennae and long legs ideal for running. The females are larger than the males.

HABITS & HABITAT Found in a wide range of habitats, but especially abundant at the edges of Rift Valley lakes, including alkaline (soda) lakes and rivers in hot, arid regions. They move swiftly, taking flight when approached. Males are often found riding on the backs of females, while copulating.

A. POWYS

Diving beetles DYSTICIDAE

5–50mm A highly diverse group of aquatic beetles. They have elegant, very streamlined, oval-shaped bodies. Colour varies depending on species, from green to brown, but they are always smooth and shiny. The hind legs are very well developed, with hairs that aid in swimming.

HABITS & HABITAT Voracious predators that move swiftly and efficiently through the water, surfacing periodically to breathe: they capture a bubble of air (to serve as a supply of oxygen) and then dive back down with it. They fly at night and are drawn to lights, but then fall to the ground and move about in noisy circles. They feed on aquatic insects, tadpoles and small fish.

M.N. MUTISO

Large whirligig beetles GYRINIDAE

~20mm Medium-sized, very streamlined but flattened insects. Body is typically shiny black, sometimes with metallic reflections. The distinctive compound eyes are divided into two, with part of the eye seeing above the water and the other half of the eye looking down into the water!

HABITS & HABITAT They move on the surfaces of flowing streams and rivers, where they tend to occur singly or in small groups. Sometimes found resting on floating vegetation. They feed on small insects that become trapped on the surface of the water, but also scavenge opportunistically.

Small whirligig beetles GYRINIDAE

~10mm Small, streamlined, flattened insects. Generally black with shiny reflections, sometimes with a margin that varies in colour between different species. The tip of the abdomen projects beyond the wing cases. They have divided eyes, short antennae and powerful legs.

HABITS & HABITAT As the name suggests, groups of these beetles whirl madly about at dizzying speed on the surface of the water. They tend to occur in groups. Highly gregarious and nervous, they will whizz about in an almost crazy fashion when approached or disturbed. Predators and scavengers of small insects.

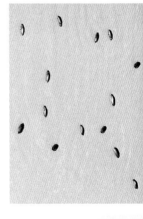

Hister beetles

HISTERIDAE

5–10mm Generally small, rounded, compact beetles. Bodies hard and smooth, usually dark blackish or brownish and shiny. The elytra don't cover the entire abdomen – the tip and last segments remain visible.

HABITS & HABITAT Typically found in, on or near animal dung or other rich, decaying matter. Sometimes found on carrion and in hidden places beneath bark or in decaying logs. These predators feed other small insects and larvae in the dung and carrion that they frequent.

Carrion beetles

SILPHIDAE

10–30mm Squat, heavily built insects with somewhat flattened bodies that are rather soft, with a slightly rough texture. Colour is highly variable: species usually range from green to brown, but some are red, black or orange.

HABITS & HABITAT Specialised insects that feed primarily on carrion and are therefore found on, beneath, or in the vicinity of animal carcasses. A highly developed sense of smell allows adults to locate carcasses over long distances. In some species, males and females cooperate to bury small carcasses so as to lay eggs on them.

Soldier carrion beetles

CLERIDAE

5–10mm Generally small insects found on the decomposing carcasses of mammals. They are elongate, slightly flattened in shape, with straight, parallel sides. The body is typically a shiny, reflective, metallic green. The eyes are darker and the legs are sometimes orange or brown.

HABITS & HABITAT Found on the carcasses of mammals in bush and savanna regions. Especially visible on carcasses of cattle, elephants or other large animals left to rot in the open. Can be found crawling over exposed bones that are covered in membranes, where they mate and lay eggs in tiny cavities.

Rove beetles

STAPHYLINIDAE

2–20mm Generally small, furtive beetles with very narrow, elongated bodies. The elytra are short, leaving most of the abdomen exposed and visible. Colour variable – most are dark and metallic, but some are metallic red or blue.

HABITS & HABITAT Common and widespread in many kinds of habitat, but generally associated with moist habitats with rich decaying matter, leaf litter, dung or carrion. Often found in the vicinity of springs, including hot springs. They prey on other insects and some are scavengers. Biology poorly understood. Known for curling the abdomen over the back.

Nairobi eyes

Paederus spp.

5–7mm Among the more distinctive rove beetles. The narrow body is boldly marked in red and dark metallic blue and can appear almost black. The abdomen is visible, as the wings are short and do not cover the back.

HABITS & HABITAT Common name 'Nairobi eye' derives from outbreaks of severe blistering caused by the toxins released when one of these beetles lands on human skin. The toxins (pederin) are produced by bacteria living in the beetle. Often mistakenly called 'Nairobi fly'. Common and widespread, especially after rains. Drawn to lights.

Stag beetles

LUCANIDAE

40–60mm Large insects, and among the most striking East African beetles. Males have massively enlarged mandibles (inset). Most East African species are tan, rich yellow-brown or beige, but some are black or orange. Females are smaller, less heavily built and lack the large mandibles.

HABITS & HABITAT Rare and localised insects of rainforest and woodland areas. Often seen when drawn to fermenting fruit or sap, or found sunning themselves on logs in forests. Larvae feed inside fallen, decaying logs, often taking many years to develop.

Rose chafers
Pachnoda spp.

20–30mm Members of this group are familiar and striking, with robust, oblong, hard, smooth bodies. Colour variable, typically variations of black and ochre-yellow, with red-brown wings, sometimes spotted. Undersides often a different colour to wings.

HABITS & HABITAT Among the most recognisable of East African insects, ubiquitous in gardens, in cultivation and in other areas throughout the region. Most often seen resting and feeding on flowers in gardens, including roses and other cultivated species. Larvae live in rich matter, including manure or compost.

Zig-zag fruit chafers
Anisorrhina spp.

~25mm A shiny, striking and elegant beetle. The body is smooth. It is rich orange-brown, with a few variable black spots, and the elytra have bold yellow markings. Eyes black. Has short, clubbed antennae.

HABITS & HABITAT Fairly common in suitable habitats, it is generally found in warm coastal regions on flowering shrubs and fruiting trees, including in gardens, woodlands and bush. Known to enter beehives. Flies noisily and clumsily, and is easily captured by hand. The larvae develop in rich dung or manure piles.

Small green flower chafers
SCARABAEIDAE

10–15mm A widespread group of highly variable bright emerald green and black or emerald green and red beetles. Body hard, smooth, shiny and somewhat metallic, with variable white or pale spots on the elytra. They have short, clubbed antennae.

HABITS & HABITAT Common and widespread in bush, savanna, grassland and woodland habitats, especially after the rains have begun and herbaceous wildflowers have started blooming. They feed on flowers, often despoiling and fouling them. Attracted to fermenting fruit and other ripe, sweet-smelling matter.

Emerald fruit chafers
Rhabdotis spp.

20–30mm Medium-sized insects with robust, oblong bodies that range from bright green to olive green, with a metallic sheen. The legs are covered in pale hairs. There are white spots on the elytra and body, which vary in number and shape. They have short, clubbed antennae.
HABITS & HABITAT Abundant and familiar insects that occur in gardens and most habitats across the region. Adults typically found feeding greedily on flowers, often mating and moving about. Common on flowering trees, including crotons, acacias and garden shrubs. Also attracted to fermenting fruit and to sap on trees.

Dotted fruit chafers
SCARABAEIDAE

~10mm Members of this group are widespread and highly variable. Typically have small, compact, black or blackish bodies, with variable white spots on the wings and thorax. Several closely related and similar white-spotted species are common in the region.
HABITS & HABITAT They feed voraciously and in large numbers on flowers in gardens and in the bush. Often found mating on flowers while feeding. Some species can be pests in gardens, causing damage to ornamental flowers, but are easily controlled using fruit- or alcohol-baited traps.

Small fruit chafers
SCARABAEIDAE

~10mm Members of this group are widespread and highly variable. They have small, well-built, slightly smooth bodies. Brightly coloured and variable, they may be any combination of black, orange, red or yellow.
HABITS & HABITAT Common and widespread visitors to flowering trees and shrubs in many different habitats. They tend to favour moist areas, especially woodland and forest edges, but also gardens. There are many similar related species, including some that are uniformly coloured.

Striped goliath beetles
Goliathus spp.

50–60mm Large, elegant, striking insects. The body is rugged, heavily built, with long, nimble legs, a narrow head, a beautiful rounded thorax and oblong elytra. The thorax and wings have variable white or cream patterns on a dark background.

HABITS & HABITAT An unmistakable insect of moist woodland, coastal bush, savanna and gallery forest. Adults are attracted to fermenting sap and fruit. They sometimes fly noisily into bush camps. Commonly found in warm low-altitude regions, but also in riverine forest in highland areas.

Emerald goliath beetles
Mecynorrhina spp.

45–55mm Large, elegant and striking insects. The body is smooth, beautifully metallic and shiny. Males have pronounced heads with short horns; females have more rounded heads. Colour variable, but typically shiny green with hints of gold and orange and some black.

HABITS & HABITAT Can be fairly common, but generally restricted to forest and woodland in tropical regions in the west. Often seen flying clumsily into trees, attracted to fermenting sap. Will sometimes become 'drunk' when feeding on sap, falling to the ground or bumping into trees in flight.

M N MUTISO

Giant goliath beetle
Goliathus goliathus

100–120mm The heaviest insect in the world. A massive, unmistakable, handsome beetle. Head and thorax have black and white stripes, and males have short horns. The wings are a deep, rich red-brown. They have long, elegant, nimble black legs.

HABITS & HABITAT Localised and fairly rare; found in rainforests in western Kenya, Uganda and far western Tanzania. Breathtaking to watch as they fly noisily through the canopy. They are drawn to fermenting fruit and sap. The larvae are massive grubs that develop slowly in rotting logs over many years.

Rhinoceros beetles
Oryctes spp.

40–50mm Large, obvious and easily recognised beetles. Adult males have a long, curved horn on their heads. Females are smaller and lack this horn. The body is rich red-brown, very shiny, hard and smooth. They have strong legs and short, clubbed antennae.

HABITS & HABITAT These beetles are fairly common and widespread, especially in habitats where palm trees grow, including riverine forest and woodland. Mostly seen at night, when they fly clumsily into lights and fall to the ground. The larvae are grubs (inset) that feed in rotting vegetation.

E.M. GITONGA (BOTH)

Brown chafers
SCARABAEIDAE

5–20mm A familiar, common, highly variable group of chafers whose members are typically uniform pale brown or tan. They have oblong, smooth, fairly hard bodies, rounded heads and gangly legs.

HABITS & HABITAT These are among the most abundant insects in the region during the rainy season. Huge numbers emerge periodically after rain in woodland, bush and dryland areas, attracted to lights in their thousands. Widely known as 'toast' or potato beetles. The larvae are grubs that live in soil, among roots.

Small dung beetles
SCARABAEIDAE

~10mm Tiny, compact and attractive dung beetles. Highly variable depending on the species. Many are elegant and shiny, in various shades of metallic green or brown. Depending on the species, males may have anything from one to several horns on their head.

HABITS & HABITAT Fairly common and widespread in bush, savanna, woodland and forest habitats. They actively seek out the dung of mammals, including the small dung pellets of antelope and the dung of primates and carnivores. The group includes species that roll balls of dung away and those that simply excavate tunnels beneath dung.

Sacred dung beetle · *Kheper aegyptiorum*

35–40mm Elegant, robust and rotund beetles that are familiar and widespread. Broad and somewhat flattened, with dark bodies that have greenish or purplish metallic glints. The front legs are strong and toothed for digging.
HABITS & HABITAT They occur in grassland and savanna habitats across East Africa, where browsing mammals and large herds of grazers occur. Seasonally abundant. Drawn to fresh dung, where they can be found frantically rolling balls. Males and females are monogamous and provide parental care to their larvae inside underground burrows.

Scarab dung beetles · *Scarabaeus* spp.

25–30mm Chunky, robust, dung beetles with flattened bodies. Usually dull black, but can appear grey, brown or reddish if covered in dung or dust. They have deep grooves in their wings. Their long, curved hind legs provide grip when they roll dung balls, while the short, reduced forelegs are used for digging and shaping dung.
HABITS & HABITAT Common and widespread in bush, grassland and savanna habitats in association with large mammals, including cattle. Males roll nuptial balls for courting, and females are often found riding on a suitor's ball. Important for removing dung, limiting breeding of biting flies and helping to disperse seeds.

Giant dung beetles · *Heliocopris* spp.

55–65mm Massive, robust dung beetles. Among the heaviest of East African insects. Typically a deep, rich red-brown, with shiny wings and thorax. Males usually have short horns on the head and thorax; females lack horns.
HABITS & HABITAT Fairly widespread and seasonally common insects in savanna and bush in Kenya and Tanzania. Associated with elephant dung and rhino middens, they dig tunnels beneath piles of dung, where they stash brood balls, each one containing a single, massive, slow-growing larva that eventually pupates and hatches out.

Giant jewel beetles *Sternocera* spp.

40–50mm A large, striking beetle. The body is robust, especially around the thorax, and the abdomen tapers to a blunt point. The elytra are dark greenish-black, with fine speckling and pale yellow patches.

HABITS & HABITAT Fairly common and widespread in bush and savanna habitats. Most often found clinging to tree trunks or taking off noisily from flowering acacias and other trees. Flight loud and clumsy. The larvae live underground and feed on the roots of trees.

Painted jewel beetles BUPRESTIDAE

20–30mm Flashy, medium to large insects with large, shiny black eyes. The body is very hard, varying from bright green to brown, with a metallic sheen, while the thorax has variable red patches. The wings have yellow and black markings, similar to the blister beetles (Meloidae).

HABITS & HABITAT Inhabitants of warm, dry and arid bush regions in the east, and along the Rift Valley. Frequently found sunning themselves on leaves in bushes during the rainy season, sometimes in association with blister beetles. Often play dead when handled or bothered, dropping unceremoniously to the ground.

Brown jewel beetles BUPRESTIDAE

20–40mm A widespread and common group of jewel beetles. Size varies depending on the species. Body is robust and tapering, ranging in colour from pale tan or soft beige to ochre-yellow and brown. The elytra are very hard and sharp.

HABITS & HABITAT Common and seasonally abundant jewel beetles. Well known and often seen after rains in acacia-dominated woodland, bush and savanna habitats. The Maasai of southern Kenya and northern Tanzania use the wing cases to make necklaces (inset).

F. SMITH

Water pennies   PSEPHENIDAE

5–10mm Smallish, distinctive, aquatic beetles.
The larvae are more often noticed than the
adults: they are extremely flattened, circular or
oval and may be found clinging tightly to rocks.
Their colour varies, depending on the species,
from pale ivory with orange markings to brown
with some darker mottling and patterning. Adults
are compact, slow-moving brown beetles.
HABITS & HABITAT Aquatic insects found in
rocky streams and rivers. Widespread, though
often overlooked, in most unpolluted streams
and rivers across the region.

M N MUTISO

Giant click beetles   ELATERIDAE

50–80mm Large and distinctive beetles. Smooth,
elegant, with very hard bodies, which are
covered in hairs that often wear or scratch off to
reveal a shiny, almost metallic, polished-looking
surface. Edges of thorax pointed. A special
notch and pointed spine on the underside can
be 'clicked' in a rapid, defensive motion.
HABITS & HABITAT As the name indicates, can
violently snap the edge of the unique spine-
notch mechanism. The edges of the thorax can
pinch fingers (otherwise harmless). Associated
with acacia woodland and savanna.

Brown click beetles   ELATERIDAE

20–30mm A highly variable and widespread
group of click beetles. Generally small to
medium-sized, with compact, streamlined, very
hard bodies. Colour pale to darkish-brown; often
has hairs that rub off easily, giving the beetle a
slightly 'worn-out' look. Antennae variable.
HABITS & HABITAT Common and abundant
insects, especially in areas with acacias,
including plantations of exotic wattles in the
highlands of Kenya and Uganda. Also seasonally
common in drylands, including hot, arid areas
with *Acacia tortilis* trees. Typically found
crawling on bark. They move fairly slowly, but
will fly away if disturbed.

Fireflies/glowworms LAMPYRIDAE

5–35mm Variable but highly recognisable.
Adults are mobile, soft-bodied, narrowly built
insects with large black eyes and dark wings.
The thorax is orange-brown and the underside is
paler orange. The tip of the abdomen can flash
a greenish-yellow light. The larvae are flattened
brown grubs with bioluminescent spots or a
bioluminescent tip to the abdomen.

HABITS & HABITAT Typically noticed at dusk or
at night, when adults can be found flying and
flashing in moist habitats. In fireflies (which are
actually beetles, main image), both sexes fly
around and flash at each other. In glowworms,
only the males can fly; females remain wingless.
Larvae (inset) prey on molluscs. Adults are
scavengers but also cannibalise other fireflies.

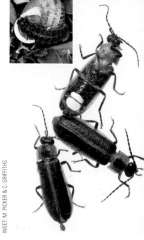

INSET: M. PICKER & C. GRIFFITHS

Large net-winged beetles LYCIDAE

20–25mm Distinctive insects that are common
and widespread. Wings are rounded and
beautifully shaped. Colour generally a rich tan-
orange with variable black markings or patches,
especially towards the wing tips. Name 'net-
winged' refers to the fine, net-like veins that are
visible in the wings on close observation.

HABITS & HABITAT Gentle, slow-moving,
confident insects that are a classic example
of warning colouring, as the beetles contain
noxious chemicals to deter predators. Active
during the day and often found on grasses
or flowers.

Slender net-winged beetles LYCIDAE

10–20mm Small beetles with narrow, elongate
bodies. Wings are a rich orange, with black tips.
Veins elaborate, but only seen on close inspection.
Antennae are serrated, black, and fairly long,
typically held arched out from the head.

HABITS & HABITAT Common and sometimes
ubiquitous insects in bush, savanna, forest,
woodland and gardens throughout East Africa.
Bold patterns are a warning signal and mimicked
by a number of other insects including longhorn
beetles (Cerambycidae). They move slowly and
their flight is also slow and awkward.

M.N. MUTISO

Groove-winged flower beetles

MELYRIDAE

~5mm Small, common and widespread beetles. The body and wings typically appear rough and finely pitted, with a dull metallic sheen. In East Africa mostly green, but colour can vary from bronze-green to blue-green to copper or purplish. **HABITS & HABITAT** Seasonally abundant and ubiquitous insects in grassland, bush and savanna habitats. Most often found in large numbers on the flowers of members of the daisy family (Asteraceae), acacias, euphorbias and others. Males and females often found mating on flowers, with males clinging onto females' backs.

Ladybird beetle larvae COCCINELLIDAE

~5mm These strange and distinctive larval ladybird beetles are often mistaken for other species. They have elongate bodies, with a soft, slightly pudgy or fleshy texture and appearance and are covered with blunt, triangular protuberances. They are blackish-grey in colour, with pale markings. **HABITS & HABITAT** Among the most useful of all insects, as they are common and widespread predators of aphids, including those that afflict several crops. They offer a very efficient form of natural pest control.

E.M. GITONGA

Lunate ladybirds *Cheilomenes* spp.

~7mm Familiar and endearing. Adults are unmistakable, with black and red (sometimes yellow) markings. Size and patterning of the red patches varies. They have smooth, shiny elytra and the head is black and yellow. **HABITS & HABITAT** Common and widespread. These engaging insects are often picked up and admired. Found in many different types of vegetation (except in very dry areas). They are especially abundant in fields of cultivated Rhodes grass (*Chloris* spp.). Used widely for biological control in greenhouses and gardens.

Striped ladybirds

COCCINELLIDAE

5–7mm Common and widespread insects.
Adults are highly variable beetles, with a
generally pale background colour and black, red
or orange stripes. The wings are smooth and
shiny and the body is compact and circular. The
legs are often tucked in under the body.
HABITS & HABITAT Ubiquitous insects
of grasslands and most gardens. Can be
seasonally abundant and often noticed by
people walking through flowering grass.
Voracious predators, both as adults and larvae,
feeding on aphids and other small herbivorous
insects (primarily true bugs, Hemiptera).

E.M. GITONGA

Nightshade (potato) ladybirds

Epilachna spp.

8–10mm Medium-sized ladybird beetles with
a slightly fuzzy appearance because of the
fine white down that covers the wings. Colour
varies, but is usually dull red or pinkish. Wings
have black spots or patterns, the size and
number of which vary with species.
HABITS & HABITAT Common and widespread in
most suitable habitats. Unlike their relatives, these
ladybirds are pests, feeding on plants including
cultivated potatoes, tomatoes and other members
of the Solanaceae family. In the wild found on
Solanum spp. They feed slowly and methodically
on leaves, skeletonising them in the process.

Mouldy beetles

Eurychora spp.

10–12mm Medium-sized, more or less oval
beetles. Adults are distinguished by the layer of
sand, dried plant material and other debris that
covers and camouflages the back. This debris is
held in place by hairs and other long filaments
protruding from the elytra.
HABITS & HABITAT Sluggish, shy and typically
nocturnal beetles. Found moving slowly
around in rock shelters, the burrows of various
animals and in dark, sheltered rooms in huts
and houses. Usually freezes and plays dead
when touched.

BEETLES   67

Warty stone beetles
TENEBRIONIDAE

10–20mm Medium-sized beetles with a stocky, portly build. The body is robust and very, very hard with an almost indestructible exoskeleton. The wings are fused and covered with rough lumps and blunt protuberances. They are blackish-brown, but often look the colour of soil due to the accumulation of dust on the rough surfaces of the body.

HABITS & HABITAT Ubiquitous, slow-moving, ponderous beetles that are typically found scurrying over bare ground. They immediately freeze when approached or handled, playing dead for some time. Omnivorous scavengers.

Tree darkling beetles
TENEBRIONIDAE

15–25mm A group of distinctive and beautiful Tenebrionid beetles. Medium-sized insects that have a rather bulbous, almost inflated appearance. The body is shiny and metallic, in various greenish or purplish shades, depending on the species.

HABITS & HABITAT Fairly common in wet woodland and tropical forest. Often found clinging to the trunks of rough-barked trees in glades or hillsides within forests. Little is known of their biology in tropical Africa, but they are probably scavengers. As with other darkling beetles, they are shy and immediately freeze and drop to the ground if touched.

Large blister beetles
Mylabris spp.

25–30mm Large, striking and noticeable blister beetles. The head and thorax are black and shiny and the eyes are bright and black. The antennae are often bright orange. Wings boldly striped with variable bands of pale yellow or bright red. There are a number of related species.

HABITS & HABITAT Typically found perched on flowers or leaves in a prominent position to display their warning colours. They produce a toxin that can blister human skin. Unafraid, remaining in place even when approached. They feed on flowers, sometimes damaging plants in gardens. The larvae are parasites of various insects, including bees and grasshoppers.

Lunate blister beetles   MELOIDAE

10–15mm Medium-sized beetles that are
widespread and common. Body colour is
typically black or blackish, with variable bands
of yellow. Head rounded, with bright eyes and
a distinctly narrow neck. The antennae are
curved, with thickened tips.

HABITS & HABITAT Ubiquitous on flowers of
many different plants, in a wide range of habitats.
Can be seasonally very abundant, and most often
noticed on showy flowers, such as morning
glories, as they despoil them. As with all blister
beetles, they are capable of secreting highly toxic
cantharidin, which can blister human skin.

Carpenter bee blister beetles

Synhoria spp.

25–35mm A large, striking and somewhat
fearsome-looking beetle. Head, thorax and elytra
are a uniform angry bright red. Eyes, antennae
and legs are black. In males the mandibles are
very large, curved, sharp and dagger-like.

HABITS & HABITAT The larvae are specialised
parasites of the nests of carpenter bees
(*Xylocopa* spp.). Adult beetles are most often
found crawling about slowly in the vicinity of
carpenter bee nests. Often seen on wooden
verandahs, old, drying logs and in other areas
where their hosts make nests.

Metallic longhorns   *Promeces* spp.

15–20mm Medium-sized, striking and beautiful
insects. Narrow-bodied, with a slender, elegant
build. Head, thorax and wings are a shiny,
metallic emerald green. The antennae are black,
curve outward and are longer than the body.

HABITS & HABITAT Larvae are woodboring
creatures, often associated with shrubs in bush,
woodland, savanna and grassland areas. Adults
are typically seen feeding on yellow flowers
of members of the daisy family (Asteraceae),
including *Aspilia* (image shows mating pair).
Most often noticed in grassland after rains,
where they can be very common.

Banded longhorns
CERAMBYCIDAE

25–40mm Striking, medium to large insects with the elegant black antennae typical of longhorn beetles. The wings have dull red bands that vary in width and intensity of colour. In some species the wings have dull red speckling.

HABITS & HABITAT Common, widespread and often-noticed insects of forest, woodland, bush and savanna habitats. Most often encountered sunning themselves on tree leaves or trunks. The larvae are woodborers that feed inside dying or drying branches and can be pests of timber plantations in some areas.

Giant longhorns
Tithoes spp.

60–95mm Huge, somewhat terrifying-looking beetles. The head, body and wings are dark brown with variable mottling that results from hairs rubbing off their surfaces. The sides of the thorax have short, sharp spines. Bears large, sharp, powerful mandibles.

HABITS & HABITAT Primarily nocturnal, they are most often seen when drawn to lights, sometimes flying violently into them and crashing to the ground. The larvae are huge, bulbous grubs that bore through a wide range of trees, including cultivated mangoes, cashews and other trees. Common and widespread.

Wasp-mimicking longhorns
CERAMBYCIDAE

10–35mm A variable and widespread group of longhorn beetles. Typically black or blackish, with a number of yellow, orange and red patches, spots and other markings. Elegant, beautiful insects that are quite easily spotted.

HABITS & HABITAT Fairly common and widespread in suitable habitats. They tend to be found more in savanna, woodland and forest areas, where it is thought that they mimic large pompilid wasps. Confident in their deceit, and can easily be picked up from leaves where they are often found sunning themselves.

Metallic leaf beetles CHRYSOMELIDAE

~10mm Common and widespread beetles. Highly variable, depending on the species. Most are small to medium-sized, deep metallic blue insects, with green or purple reflections. They have long antennae relative to their bodies, and prominent eyes.
HABITS & HABITAT A ubiquitous group of beetles found seasonally on a wide range of plants in drylands, bush and savanna regions. Often found resting on the leaves, thorns and flowers of aloes, acacias and many other plant species. Although they are very common, little is known of their biology other than that they are herbivorous.

Spiny leaf beetles *Dicladispa* spp.

~10mm Common and widespread beetles. Mostly small and squat with long antennae and legs relative to their compact bodies. Usually brown and blackish. Wings are distinctive, covered with untidy, short, prickly spines.
HABITS & HABITAT A ubiquitous group of beetles seen during the rains on a wide range of plants in different habitats, and often found resting on leaves or foliage in gardens and shambas. Though widespread, their biology is poorly studied. The larvae are thought to be primarily leaf miners, feeding inside leaf tissues.

Furry leaf beetles CHRYSOMELIDAE

5–10mm A widespread and familiar group of beetles. Size and colour vary depending on species, but they are typically greenish or olive with long, slightly thickened antennae (relative to the body) and some hairs on the wings.
HABITS & HABITAT Ubiquitous and abundant in cultivated areas and in grassland, woodland and forest throughout East Africa. Most often noticed when feeding on the leaves of vegetables in gardens or on farms. These beetles are generally sedentary and feed slowly and methodically on leaves. They drop to the ground or freeze if touched or startled.

Circular tortoise beetles
Aspidimorpha spp.

7–10mm Beautiful beetles, often seen on vegetation. Instantly recognisable by their circular, flattened shape, and the partly transparent edges to both wings and thorax. The head is hidden from view below the thorax (pronotum).

HABITS & HABITAT Common and widespread in moist habitats, including gardens, woodlands and forest edges. Typically associated with plants of the tomato/potato family (Solanaceae) and with morning glories (*Ipomoea* spp.). The larvae are strange, elongate and spiny and hold faecal pellets above their backs for camouflage.

Silver tortoise beetles
CHRYSOMELIDAE

~10mm One of East Africa's most beautiful insects. Adults are almost perfectly circular when viewed from above, with a beautiful, metallic silver lustre that changes in intensity with the light. Edges of wings and thorax are translucent.

HABITS & HABITAT Fairly common in forest and moist habitats in the west of the region. Adults are typically found moving about on the foliage of morning glories, at the edges of forest or in riverine areas. They tend to freeze, tucking in their heads and legs if startled, while holding fast to the leaf where they were feeding.

Bruchid beetles
BRUCHIDAE

2–5mm Tiny beetles that are most often overlooked, but that are evident from the damage they cause to seeds. Adults are compact, slightly rotund, with an oval shape. Colour is typically brownish or black, with variable mottling, hairs and patterning on wings.

HABITS & HABITAT Common and widespread, and mostly seen as pests of stored beans, green gram, dhal and other legumes. In the wild, found in the pods of most acacias and related species. Among the most important seed predators, as they infest and compromise the viability of large quantities of seeds.

Maize (grain) weevils · *Sitophilus* spp.

~5mm These small weevils are familiar, if unwelcome, to most people in East Africa. Adults are elongate, slightly oval-shaped with a distinctive long snout that is visible to the naked eye on close inspection. They are dark brown and red.

HABITS & HABITAT Among the most common, widespread and well-known insects wherever cereals, especially maize and rice, are grown. In East Africa they are primarily associated with stored maize in silos, granaries and homesteads. Have a huge economic impact, as they can consume up to four in every 10 harvested bags of maize if left unchecked.

Leaf-feeding weevils · *Sciobius* spp.

~10mm Elegant, common weevils. Smallish, fairly stout and robust, with elongate snouts. Their bodies are dark, with pale hairs or grooves that appear to be stripes. Legs fairly long, with slightly thickened tarsi, used for holding onto leaves.

HABITS & HABITAT One of the most abundant groups of weevils in East Africa. Its members are common in gardens, woodlands, along forest margins and other habitats during the rains. Larvae feed on tree roots, including those of several fruit trees. Adults most often found feeding on leaves. Some species are pests in plantations of eucalyptus (inset).

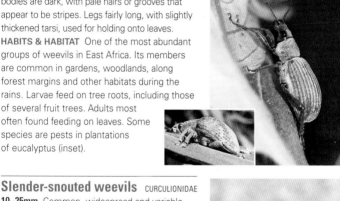

Slender-snouted weevils · CURCULIONIDAE

10–25mm Common, widespread and variable weevils. All species have a fairly long and slender snout with mandibles at the tip. Antennae are fairly long with a distinct 'elbow' joint halfway. Colour variable, usually brownish.

HABITS & HABITAT Abundant insects in a wide range of habitats. Often seen moving about or sunning themselves on leaves, logs or paths. Insides of legs and feet have strong hooks for gripping surfaces, and this sometimes makes them hold fast to fingers when handled. Harmless. Biology little known.

Elegant weevils
CURCULIONIDAE

10–30mm Size and colour highly variable depending on the species. They have rotund, stocky bodies. Usually pale with tan, beige, pink, yellow or other hairs. The snout is fairly long. Their antennae have 'elbow' joints and are thicker at the tips.

HABITS & HABITAT Fairly common and widespread weevils in woodland, forest and the warmer, wetter parts of East Africa. Some species found feeding on crops, but most are encountered on foliage along trails in woodland or forested areas. Weevils are among the largest and most diverse insect groups, yet remain poorly studied.

Green leaf weevils
CURCULIONIDAE

10–30mm Size and colour highly variable depending on the species. Have fairly robust, pear-shaped bodies. May be various shades of green, often metallic. The snout is fairly long. Their antennae have 'elbow' joints and are thicker at the tips.

HABITS & HABITAT Fairly common and widespread in woodland, forest and the warmer, wetter parts of East Africa. These weevils are mostly encountered on foliage along trails. Slow-moving and ponderous, they will drop to the ground if bothered.

Straight-snouted weevils
BRENTIDAE

30–50mm Also known as giraffe weevils or brentid weevils. A variable but distinctive group whose members have very elongate, slender and straight-sided bodies. The head, snout, elytra and legs are long and thin. Their antennae look beaded. Colour varies, but is usually brownish with orange, red and black. The wings (elytra) are often finely grooved.

HABITS & HABITAT A fairly widespread group of weevils. They are shy, gentle and retiring insects. Biology poorly studied, but adults are often found beneath the bark of old forest logs and trees, where they use their snouts to bore holes in which to lay eggs.

Crane flies TIPULIDAE

10–65mm A variable, but unmistakable group of flies. Adults are gangly, long-legged creatures (often called daddy-longlegs). Wings clear, sometimes with faint markings. Body colour varies from orange to black or brown.
HABITS & HABITAT Ubiquitous, most often found in or near buildings at lights, or resting on foliage. Larvae are elongate, worm-like creatures that live in seasonal pools, damp soil and other moist habitats. The gangly appearance of these insects often causes people to fear them, but they are completely harmless.

Moth flies PSYCHODIDAE

~5mm Generally small flies. Easily recognised by their fuzzy bodies and broad, rounded wings, which have a hairy appearance. Antennae are finely serrated. Usually grey or blackish in colour. Overall, they resemble small moths.
HABITS & HABITAT Widespread and familiar insects, most often seen in bathrooms, showers or other damp areas, where they can be found perched on walls. They breed in drains and sewage, where they perform the invaluable function of eating through thick mats of algae that would otherwise clog these areas. The related sand flies are the vector for leishmaniasis in East Africa.

Midges/gnats CHIRONOMIDAE

5–12mm Common and widespread insects. Adults are often mistaken for mosquitoes, but most don't bite people. They have narrow bodies, and the wings are folded over the back at rest. Colour variable: blackish, brown or grey and often striped.
HABITS & HABITAT Ubiquitous and seasonally abundant insects. Adults are very short-lived, and are most often noticed in frantic mating swarms or dying around lights in houses. The larvae of several common species are the aquatic 'bloodworms' found either in stagnant water bodies with rotting vegetation or in heavily polluted water.

Elephant mosquitoes   *Toxorhynchetes* spp.

15–20mm Large, elegant and beautiful mosquitoes. Their very noticeable, well-developed, biting mouthparts form a proboscis. Colour is blue-black and white with variable silvery, iridescent scales or spots. They have long black-and-white striped legs.

HABITS & HABITAT A fairly common and widespread species in forest, woodland and other moist habitats. They do not feed on blood and are therefore not vectors of disease. The larvae live in tree holes and other such locations and feed on other mosquito larvae. They are thus a useful form of natural control over vector species, especially grass mosquitoes.

House mosquito larvae   *Culex* spp.

5–10mm Common and widespread mosquito larvae. They are brownish, slightly patterned, worm-like, swimming larvae, with a distinctive fan-like breathing apparatus. They hang and swim at an angle in water, surface to breathe, and then wriggle away.

HABITS & HABITAT Among the most common mosquito larvae associated with human habitation. They breed in a wide range of natural and man-made water bodies. Can often be found in very large numbers in water tanks, sewage tanks and rainwater barrels. Often noticed swimming in large groups when tanks are inspected.

House mosquitoes   *Culex* spp.

8–10mm A group of widespread, common and familiar mosquitoes. They are small and perch parallel to the surfaces they land on. Typically brownish with paler stripes, scales or spots. Eyes greenish if viewed up close.

HABITS & HABITAT Perhaps the most abundant of all mosquitoes associated with human dwellings. Most typically encountered indoors, where they shelter in corners, behind curtains and under furniture. They actively bite people and other animals. Not an important vector, but can transmit lymphatic filariasis.

Grass mosquitoes
Aedes spp.

6–10mm Common and familiar mosquitoes, also known as bush mosquitoes or grass mozzies. They have elegant, boldly patterned, striking black bodies with bright silver-white stripes and spots. The legs are long and similarly striped.

HABITS & HABITAT Among the most common and widespread of all mosquitoes. They bite during the day and, especially, in the evenings, but not at night. Bites are often quite itchy and swell up slightly. Grass mosquitoes are the vectors for yellow fever (very rare in the region), dengue fever (along the coast), and sometimes for the worms responsible for lymphatic filariasis (elephantiasis).

Malaria mosquito larvae
Anopheles spp.

7–10mm Fairly common and widespread mosquito larvae. They are pale brown and speckled, often well camouflaged and aquatic. The larvae swim parallel to the surface using breathing tubes on their tails to access air. Parallel orientation to the surface when in the water is a diagnostic feature of malaria mosquito larvae.

HABITS & HABITAT Common in all warm, low-altitude regions of East Africa. Typically found in puddles, ponds, pools, wells along swamp edges and in other stagnant water bodies. They graze on algae and often flee to the bottom of the water body if startled.

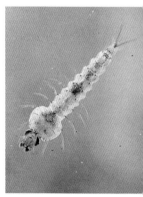

Malaria mosquitoes
Anopheles spp.

7–10mm Among the most important vectors of disease worldwide. Small, extremely sleek and slender mosquitoes with prominent, slightly thickened mouthparts. Most malaria mosquitoes rest at an angle of 45 degrees to the surfaces they land on. Body is brownish and the wings are often lightly speckled.

HABITS & HABITAT When females feed on human blood they may transmit the *Plasmodium* parasites that cause malaria. They typically bite after dark, and spend the day sheltering in or around houses. The use of bed nets is one way to control them, as it limits bites. Walls of houses and homesteads are also treated with pesticides.

Small biting midges CERATOPOGONIDAE

2–3mm Tiny insects that are more often felt than seen! Diminutive, slightly rotund midges with clear wings that are folded flat over the back when at rest. Body colour is typically shiny or dull black, grey or brownish.

HABITS & HABITAT Common and widespread. They feed on blood and body fluids from a wide range of other creatures, including mammals, birds and even other insects (pictured here feeding from a stick insect). The larvae of many species are aquatic, but some also develop in soil. In general they are poorly studied and their biology is little known.

March flies BIBIONIDAE

10–20mm Widespread and recognisable flies. Well-built, with striking orange-red thorax (in most East African species) and black wings and body. Legs long, gangly and black. Head black and rounded, with short, thick antennae that stick out.

HABITS & HABITAT Clumsy and slow-moving, they seem inept as they land, twitching and falling about, on leaves and vehicles. Adults are often found paired in copulation on leaves or tree trunks, hence their popular name 'love bugs'. Larvae live in the soil, but their biology has been poorly studied.

Black flies SIMULIIDAE

~5mm Tiny, stocky flies that are most often felt before they are seen. Compact, with roundish wings that fold over their backs. Body colour varies depending on species, usually black or grey, but sometimes brownish.

HABITS & HABITAT Females feed on the blood of mammals, birds and other vertebrates. Can be a serious nuisance, producing very itchy, inflamed bites. One species, *Simulium damnosum*, is an important vector for river blindness in northern Uganda and Kenya. The larvae are aquatic and live in fast-flowing, oxygen-rich waters.

Soldier flies STRATIOMYIIDAE

15–25mm Medium-sized to large. Beautiful, elegant flies with a robust but streamlined build. The abdomen is straight-sided with a blunt, rounded end. Wings are held flat, folded over the back at rest. Antennae slightly thickened and close together in front of the head. Brown, black or one of many other colours, with patterns or stripes.

HABITS & HABITAT Most often found on flowers or foliage in moist areas, frequently near streams or water. Often rub their front legs together when at rest. Fairly slow-moving for flies, often crawling over flowers while feeding.

Horse flies TABANIDAE

15–50mm Medium to large biting flies. Robust and stout-bodied. Their eyes are their most distinctive feature, as they are often beautifully, almost mesmerisingly, patterned and iridescent. The wings are clear or tinted, sometimes patterned. Their mouthparts form a vicious, efficient, needle-like proboscis.

HABITS & HABITAT Common and widespread insects that are often noticed around livestock and when hiking or outdoors, as they approach noisily and try to bite. They give sharp, painful bites, eliciting a reflex response in both humans and animals.

A. POWYS

Clegs *Haematopota* spp.

20–25mm Medium-sized biting flies. Stoutly built, with a slightly elongate form and wings that fold down over the sides and back of the abdomen when at rest. Their wings are longer than their bodies. Eyes are greyish, with black markings. Thick antennae project from the front of the head and have a slightly angled elbow-like joint.

HABITS & HABITAT Common and widespread flies that seem to prefer biting mammals. Most often seen around herds of cattle, impala, hartebeest, wildebeest and other species. Their bites are sharp and painful, often causing livestock to move in irritation.

Long-tongued flies
Philoliche spp.

35–45mm Large, striking flies. Brightly coloured, orange or orange-brown with a broad black stripe that runs down the back and abdomen. The proboscis is their most distinctive feature as it is long and tapering, like a syringe pointing straight out in front of the fly. They have large, very prominent, shiny black eyes.

HABITS & HABITAT They feed from both livestock and flowers. They approach livestock rather noisily, often causing animals to twitch or react in alarm. Can be found feeding from tubular flowers, including *Ipomoea* and *Convolvulus* spp. Fairly common in areas of warm, moist bush, grassland and savanna during the rainy season.

Woolly bee flies
BOMBYLIIDAE

10–15mm Small to medium-sized bee flies. Fuzzy and rather portly, their thick, fur-like coats give them a cute, teddy bear-like appearance. They have small heads, with eyes that face forward and a short, pointed proboscis.

HABITS & HABITAT Active, familiar flies that are often seen on sunny days, basking or hovering near flowers. Superbly designed for hovering, and can feed deftly from flowers in midair. They visit a wide range of flowers and are considered an important group of pollinating insects, especially in arid and semi-arid regions during the rainy season.

Large bee flies
Exoprosopa spp.

20–35mm Striking and unmistakable, medium to large insects. Wings are held flat, pointed away from the body, and often have black marks or patterns. The body is rounded and stocky, with a large, prominent head and rounded eyes. Their colour varies, but they are often boldly patterned and may mimic wasps or bees.

HABITS & HABITAT Active insects. Often seen basking confidently on bare ground or dry vegetation. They visit flowers, especially mass-flowering trees like acacias, at the beginning of the rains. The larvae are parasites of ground-nesting bees and wasps, although their biology in East Africa is insufficiently studied.

Robber flies ASILIDAE

15–25mm Members of this group within the
Asilidae have a striking, somewhat terrifying
look. Stocky but elongate, with bristly, almost
untidy hairs on the body and legs. Eyes very
prominent and all species have strong, often
hooked, legs, used to seize and hold onto prey,
as well as sharp, dagger-like mouthparts.
HABITS & HABITAT Voracious predators that
attack and seize prey in flight, then return
with their victim to a perch to feed. Prey are
stabbed with the proboscis and their body
liquids are sucked out. Robber flies feed on flies,
butterflies, small beetles and even bees.

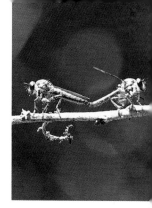

Spider-wasp robber flies ASILIDAE

20–35mm Large, robust and powerfully built
robber flies that also fall within the Asilidae.
Superb mimics of wasps, especially spider-
hunting wasps (Pompilidae). They have black
bodies, wings and legs, sometimes with orange
or yellow markings. Their legs are long and hairy,
and the eyes are prominent.
HABITS & HABITAT Widespread insects that are
often found sunning themselves in prominent
spots from which they make hunting forays. Flight
can seem a bit slow and 'buzzy', but this adds
to the impression that they are wasps. Related
species in the region are also close mimics of
various carpenter bees (*Xylocopa* spp.).

Slender robber flies *Leptogaster* spp.

~20mm Distinctive robber flies. They have
extremely thin and elongate bodies, with very
narrow abdomens and long, thin legs. The head
and thorax appear somewhat compressed
into a rounded lump. Hind legs very long, with
hooked ends.
HABITS & HABITAT A large and variable genus
in East Africa. Its members are typically found
perched on the thorns of acacias or bushes,
with the body held out at a right angle. Often
remain perched even when approached closely.
They make short flights to capture prey,
including flies and small butterflies.

A POWYS

Long-legged flies DOLICHOPODIDAE

5–10mm Members of this widespread and distinctive subfamily within the Dolichopodidae are small with long, elegant, strong legs. Males have exaggerated genitalia, often folded under the body. Colour varies from black or brown to greyish, with a shiny or metallic lustre. Eyes are prominent, often bright red, orange or iridescent.

HABITS & HABITAT Rather charming and elegant flies that move swiftly over the surfaces of leaves, where they capture and chew up a wide range of small insects. Common in moist habitats in forest and woodland regions.

Green long-legged flies DOLICHOPODIDAE

5–10mm Among the most beautiful and striking of all East African flies. Members of this subfamily within the Dolichopodidae are narrow-bodied with long, elegant legs. Usually various shades of metallic green, often with contrasting pale or dark legs. The eyes are green with multicoloured iridescent reflections.

HABITS & HABITAT Charming insects. Males often perform elaborate, somewhat comical dances on leaves, to attract females. Often found perched on leaves, where they feed on small insects. Fairly common and widespread in moist habitats (mainly forests) across the region.

Scuttle flies PHORIDAE

2–3mm Tiny, compact and fairly stocky flies. Often difficult to observe closely, as they shuffle about almost constantly. A characteristic feature is the steeply humped thorax, which gives a hunchbacked look. Colour variable – mostly black or brownish and sometimes banded. The eyes are red or dark brown.

HABITS & HABITAT Although very common, these flies may be overlooked due to their small size. Often noticed on leaves in forests, where they perform their manic dances. Some species are associated with the trails of safari ants (siafu).

Tiny hoverflies SYRPHIDAE

5–10mm Small but robust and pretty hoverflies. Colour varies depending on species, but mostly orange, yellow or black with yellow bands. Eyes large, prominent and often bright red and colourful. Wings are folded back at rest.
HABITS & HABITAT They hover in patches of sunlight in the morning, and are often active even when it is still cool. Will spend long periods of time 'holding onto' a sunny spot in midair or hovering over flowers while deciding where to find nectar. Common and widespread in all habitat types, including drylands.

Drone flies *Eristalis* spp.

~15mm Rather large, stocky and well-built hoverflies. Among the best bee mimics: with their orange-and-black banded abdomens and dark brown heads and thoraxes they closely resemble honeybees. In some species the eyes are beautifully mottled or boldly striped. The wings are held back against the sides.
HABITS & HABITAT Common and familiar insects in gardens, forests and cultivated areas. Most often seen visiting flowers, and are important pollinators of some seed crops, including carrots. The larvae are 'rat-tailed' maggots that feed on nematodes in the soil.

Banded hoverflies SYRPHIDAE

10–20mm Beautiful, elegant hoverflies. They mimic various solitary bee species. They have fairly stocky bodies, with large, prominent eyes and clear, triangular wings, which are held back against sides of the body at rest. Colour varies, but usually yellow or orange with black bands.
HABITS & HABITAT Common and widespread in grassland, bush, savanna and wooded areas. Very noticeable on mass-flowering wildflowers and trees, where they can be especially abundant. Fond of flowers in the daisy family (Asteraceae) including *Aspilia, Gutenbergia, Bidens, Vernonia, Cosmos* and related species.

Fruit flies

TEPHRITIDAE

8–10mm Small but highly noticeable flies. Stocky, with black-spotted brownish bodies. Wings held out from body at angles, variably patterned and tinted. They have short, rounded heads, and their eyes glow with iridescent reflections.

HABITS & HABITAT Among the most recognisable and widespread groups of flies. Common wherever fruit trees are grown. Two different species from the genus *Ceratitis*, the Natal fruit fly and Mediterranean fruit fly, are considered pests. Females lay eggs in fleshy fruits, which develop into maggots that feed within the fruit, spoiling it.

Milkweed fruit flies

Didacus spp.

~10mm Distinctive, striking and colourful fruit flies. Thought to be generalised mimics of small paper wasps. They have fairly robust, typically rich ochre-yellow bodies, with variable yellow markings and a narrow neck. They have prominent round heads.

HABITS & HABITAT Common and widespread wherever milkweeds *(Calotropis, Gomphocarpus* spp.) grow. Typically found perched on the inflated fruits or clustered on the undersides of leaves. They visit flowers for nectar. Closely related species include the cucurbit fly, which is a pest of watermelons, squash and pumpkins.

Red-headed flies

PLATYSTOMATIDAE

15–50mm Among the most distinctive and unforgettable flies. Size varies, depending on the species, but they are unmistakable for their bold, bright red heads and eyes, which contrast with their black bodies and wings. Squat and rather stocky. Wings are large, broadly triangular cover the abdomen and are held out from the body.

HABITS & HABITAT Typically found perched on, or in the vicinity of, decaying matter. Slow-moving and somewhat ponderous, spending long periods feeding or sitting. Though they are often noticed, very little is known about their biology in Africa.

Banana flies NERIIDAE

8–10mm One of the most recognisable true fly families. Banana flies are slender, elegant, almost robotic-looking flies. The head, thorax and abdomen are sleek and narrow. Wings are folded flat and tucked over the back at rest. Their legs are long and slightly angled.

HABITS & HABITAT Common and ubiquitous flies that are found in moist habitats including gardens, and are especially noticeable where ripening or rotting fruit accumulates, hence the common name 'banana flies'. Often found perched on tree trunks along paths in forests. Generally nervous and twitchy.

E.M. GITONGA

Stalk-eyed flies DIOPSIDAE

~10mm A bizarre and distinctive group of true flies. Their most obvious feature is their prominent eyes, which are located at the ends of long stalks, which project sideways from the head. Colour varies from black or brown to bronze, with red eyes.

HABITS & HABITAT Fairly common and widespread in areas with some water and lush vegetation, including riverine forests and swamps, as well as cultivated areas. Often found in large groups on rocks along streams, where males court females and compete with one another. The extreme eyes have evolved through sexual selection.

Black scavenger flies SEPSIDAE

~5mm Small, leggy flies that somewhat resemble ants. They have a distinctive, slightly hunched posture and long, thin legs. The body is typically black and can be metallic. The eyes are red or reddish and prominent on a round head with a narrow neck. Their wings are usually clear and are constantly waved about, even when the flies are perched.

HABITS & HABITAT Common and widespread in moist habitats, where they are often noticed on vegetation in association with dung, carrion or rotting plants near streams. Males can often be found dancing around and courting females perched on leaves.

Rock flies

LAUXANIIDAE

5–10mm Squat, slightly flattened flies with long, patterned, greyish wings that are held back, typically covering the abdomen when at rest. The eyes are bright red and prominent on an oval-shaped head. The thorax has a few obvious black bristles.

HABITS & HABITAT A common, widespread and diverse group of flies. Known as 'rock flies', as they are frequently found perched on lichen-covered rocks in riverine areas, where they shuffle about continuously, moving back and forth over the same area. Prefer damp habitats, as their larvae develop in rich, moist leaf litter.

Leaf-mining flies

AGROMYZIDAE

3–5mm A widespread group, most often recognised by the damage they cause to plants. Small to tiny flies that frequently sun themselves on foliage. Colour varies, but is usually black or brownish with a paler belly and bright red eyes. At rest, their large, clear wings are held folded neatly over the back.

HABITS & HABITAT Found in a wide range of habitats, including gardens, and cultivated areas. The adults often congregate in small numbers on foliage. The larvae are 'leaf miners' that feed inside the leaves of many different herbaceous plant species, including crops.

Vinegar flies

DROSOPHILIIDAE

3–5mm Tiny, familiar, recognisable flies. May be various combinations of brown, grey and sometimes yellow, typically with bright, prominent red eyes. *Zaprionus* spp. (shown here) have silver-white stripes on the thorax.

HABITS & HABITAT One of the most common and best known insect groups. Most often noticed at slightly overripe or ripening fruit, where they settle in large numbers, rising into the air and hovering when disturbed. The species *Drosophila melanogaster*, arguably one of the most famous insects in the world, is widely used in genetic research.

Root-maggot flies
ANTHOMYIIDAE

5–10mm Small, slender flies. Members of the common cosmopolitan genus *Anthomyia* have distinctive black-and-white stripes. Some species are grey-brown and less distinctly patterned. The legs are black and fairly long, with long, prominent black bristles. Their eyes are bright red and clearly separated on the head.
HABITS & HABITAT A common and widespread group of flies whose members are typically found in the vicinity of, or perched on, some form of rich, organic, decaying matter. The larvae of some species are serious pests of onions, cabbage, spinach and other crops.

House flies
MUSCIDAE

7–14mm Small, familiar and recognisable flies. They are fairly robust and slightly stocky, with dark stripes on the thorax and dark red eyes. They have white stripes on the sides of the head. Their legs are long and black and their wings are usually clear or very slightly tinted.
HABITS & HABITAT Very familiar insects; almost always present near humans. Adults feed on liquid, moving opportunistically between sewage, waste, faeces and uncovered food, thereby transmitting cholera, typhoid, leprosy and polio. The larvae occur in manure, rotting garbage and other household wastes.

Tsetse flies
GLOSSINIDAE

~10mm Widely recognised insects, with a wingspan of up to 25mm. Robust, slight elongate, oval-shaped and compact. The wings are tucked back and close to the body. A prominent proboscis sticks straight out from the head. Brownish, with darker mottling.
HABITS & HABITAT These flies are infamous in the region. Tsetse flies feed on blood from humans, other mammals and even reptiles and are responsible for transmitting parasitic trypanosomes, causing sleeping sickness in humans (now rare in East Africa) and nagana in livestock, which is still a serious disease. Targeted by eradication programmes in several areas. Active during the day.

Hippoboscid (lion) flies HIPPOBOSCIDAE

15–25mm Medium-sized, robust flies with squat, flattened bodies. Their wings are folded back over the abdomen at rest. They have thick, rugged legs and a broad, flat, circular thorax. Colour varies, but they are mostly brownish with paler spots or stripes. The head is small, with well-developed eyes and biting mouthparts.
HABITS & HABITAT Fairly common, especially around mammals. Frequently seen biting lions, hyenas, dogs, camels and, occasionally, humans. Related species bite cattle and one specialises on ostriches. They recover readily from being swatted. Bites are very itchy.

Blowfly maggots CALLIPHORIDAE

5–10mm Small to medium-sized grubs. These are the larval stage of bluebottles, greenbottles and blowflies. They have elongate bodies, with visible segments, and consist primarily of mouthparts and a digestive system to maximise feeding and growth.
HABITS & HABITAT The maggots hatch from large numbers of eggs laid by adult flies on the carcasses of cattle, elephants and other animals. They play an important role in cleaning up carcasses, as they form large feeding masses, secreting saliva that aids in the breakdown of the tissues. Eventually they migrate en masse from the carcass to pupate in the soil.

Copper-tailed blowflies *Chrysomya* spp.

~10mm Medium-sized flies with a wingspan of 15–18mm. Beautiful, with a shiny, metallic blue-green thorax and abdomen and a coppery sheen to the last few abdominal segments. Head has prominent, large red eyes and the wings are clear.
HABITS & HABITAT Among the most widespread and ubiquitous flies, they are often noticed on livestock, especially sheep, fresh carcasses, waste and the flowers of euphorbias and other succulents. The maggots are now used in medicine to help clean up infected wounds.

Greenbottles CALLIPHORIDAE

~10mm Medium-sized flies with a wingspan of ~20mm. Robust, fairly stout, with beautiful, shiny green bodies and clear wings. Bright red eyes almost meet on the top of the head and the face is white with a black central stripe.
HABITS & HABITAT Very common and widespread. Often the first flies to arrive at a fresh carcass, where they immediately lay eggs on the nostrils, eyes and other openings. They are important pollinators of crops, including mangoes, avocados and onions. Known to spread anthrax from carcasses, though this is rare.

Blowflies *Chrysomya* spp.

~10mm Medium-sized flies with a wingspan of ~15–20mm. Size and colouring are somewhat variable. The body is metallic blue-green and black and the wings are clear, with black-edged veins. They have large, bright red eyes and a reddish patch on the head.
HABITS & HABITAT Very common and widespread. They are attracted to carcasses and are often noticed congregating en masse on vegetation around fresh lion kills. They visit flowers in large numbers and serve as important pollinators. They breed primarily in carcasses.

Fly pirates *Bengalia* spp.

10–15mm A fairly large fly with a wingspan of 20–25mm. The body is light grey-brown with faint spots and visible bristles. The wings are slightly tinted, and the large, prominent eyes are reddish with grey mottling. Legs are black and well developed.
HABITS & HABITAT Fairly common in moist bush, savanna, woodland and forest areas. Associated with ants, which they specialise in exploiting – they steal their food but also prey directly on them. Often found perched in the vicinity of ant foraging trails, including those of safari ants (siafu) and cocktail ants (*Crematogaster* spp.).

Tachinid flies
TACHINIDAE

5–15mm A widespread and variable group of parasitic flies. Typically robust, well-built, with very large rounded heads and prominent eyes. They have short, stubby, club-like antennae at the front of the head. Colour variable, brown, black or mottled, with contrasting eyes.

HABITS & HABITAT An economically important group of flies, as their larvae are parasites of a wide range of insects. This makes them very useful in the natural biological control of plant-feeding insects. The *Alophora* sp. pictured here is a parasite of seed bugs and stink bugs (Pentatomidae).

Bollworm parasites
Dejeania spp.

10–15mm A widespread and recognisable parasitic tachinid fly. One of the 'ugliest' flies, it has a grotesque, inflated abdomen covered in untidy, thick black bristles. Usually brownish, with darker hairs and bristles.

HABITS & HABITAT Despite its appearance, this widespread fly is very important as it parasitises various moth caterpillars, including bollworms, which are serious pests. Often found perched, sunning itself on grasses, leaves or rocks and will sometimes land on backpacks, shoes and clothing during the day.

Bot flies
OESTRIDAE

10–12mm Also known as warble flies or nasal flies. Adults are stocky, with very large, round eyes. The head is almost half spherical with a wrinkled top. Colour varies, but usually dull brown or blackish with some spots and mottling.

HABITS & HABITAT Adults not often seen, but they sometimes fly into buildings or lights. The larvae are specialised parasites of mammals (including humans and livestock) and develop under the skin, causing large, hot, infected swellings. They develop slowly over many months in the host, eventually emerging to pupate in the soil.

Fleas

1–3mm Tiny insects that are especially familiar to those who keep livestock or pets. Their very robust bodies are compact and flattened for moving deftly through fur. The mouthparts are designed for piercing skin and sucking blood from their hosts.

HABITS & HABITAT Common and widespread parasites of many different animals, including domestic dogs and cats. Fleas are tenacious: their pupae form cysts that can survive very harsh conditions for long periods. They bite humans and can spread plague and typhus. They also serve as intermediate hosts for tapeworms.

M. PICKER & C. GRIFFITHS

Jiggers
Tunga spp.

1–3mm A tiny, robust and highly adapted flea. The female (inset) is a rotund, swollen mass, typically embedded in the skin of the host (main image), feeding on its blood and nutrients. Males look like typical fleas, and live free on the ground.

HABITS & HABITAT A specialised parasite that is familiar to most people in East Africa, especially in rural areas, as it burrows into the soft skin of the feet causing itchy, swollen lumps. Children are especially vulnerable, and severe infestations can have a debilitating effect in some areas. Though jiggers don't spread diseases, the wounds can become infected.

J. SEEFERMAN

EYE OF SCIENCE/SCIENCE PHOTO LIBRARY

Caddisflies
TRICHOPTERA

10–45mm Small to medium-sized, narrow-winged and narrow-bodied insects. The adults resemble small, elongate moths. Typically brown or brownish, with grey and blackish mottling in some species. They have fine antennae, usually much longer than the length of the wings and body.

HABITS & HABITAT Common and widespread in moist habitats and usually associated with flowing streams or rivers in woodland and forest. The larvae construct amazing protective cases using stones or bits of vegetation. Adults are typically seen when they approach lights. Flight is weak and feeble. Poorly studied.

Leaf roller moths TORTRICIDAE

10–15mm Also known as coddling moths. Generally small to medium-sized. The wings are folded tightly back, almost enfolding the abdomen. Colour varies with species, but they are mostly brown or grey, often speckled with other colours.

HABITS & HABITAT One of the most common and widespread groups of moths. Caterpillars roll leaves to make protective tents in which to feed. The tubes are held together with silk. Many species develop inside fruits or pods, ultimately destroying them, hence the name 'coddling moths'.

Bagworms PSYCHIDIDAE

10–40mm A unique and distinctive group of moths. The name 'bagworm' refers to the caterpillars, which construct protective cases from bits of grass, stems and even acacia thorns, tightly glued together with silk. The adult moths are pale, with elongate wings. Usually only the males fly around.

HABITS & HABITAT The caterpillars are most often noticed when moving with their distinctive cases (main image and inset). They freeze and withdraw their heads when touched or startled. They feed on many different plants, including acacias.

Flower moths SCYTHRIDIDAE

7–10mm Wingspan varies from 10–15mm. Tiny, elegant moths that often sit with their wings folded back tightly, giving a narrow, elongate outline to the body. Colour varies with species, but may be shades of brown, red, yellow or white, often spotted or striped.

HABITS & HABITAT Seasonally common and widespread in most habitats. Active during the day, these moths are often found visiting flowers, where they spend long periods perched, or sunning themselves on leaves. They eat many different kinds of plants including grasses, members of the daisy family and various legumes.

Pyralid snout moths
PYRALIDAE

7–20mm Tiny to medium-sized moths. Common and widespread, but often overlooked due to their small size. The wings and body are narrow. They often rest with the wings rolled back over the body. Usually brownish or grey-brown, sometimes with darker patches or speckling. The tiny snout projects forward.

HABITS & HABITAT Common and widespread, many species are pests of stored products and also attack crops. The caterpillars are most often noticed in homes when feeding in stored food, leaving a trail of frass (dung pellets) and strands of silk.

Burnet moths
ZYGAENIDAE

15–25mm Beautiful, elegant and colourful moths. At rest the forewings are folded back and down, covering part of the body. The antennae are fairly thick and often colourful. Their wings are metallic greenish or blue-black, sometimes with red or orange markings.

HABITS & HABITAT A striking groups of moths. Their warning coloration advertises that they are toxic, which discourages predation. The adult moths are typically found on flowers or sunning themselves on leaves. Members of genus *Saliunca* (a species of which is pictured here) are seen seasonally in drylands, where the caterpillars feed on *Cissus* spp.

Handmaidens
CTENUCHIDAE

25–30mm Elegant, conspicuous moths. Coloration varies across the many different species, but they are typically metallic blackish-green or blue, with bright red, orange or yellow patterns. Their heavy abdomens are often striped, spotted or banded with contrasting colours. The antennae are thick.

HABITS & HABITAT Most often noticed when walking through bush or grassland, where they are found clinging to stalks. Somewhat slow-moving and clumsy; also often found crawling sluggishly on the ground. Their flight is slow and fluttering.

M.N MUTISO

Small slug moths LIMACODIDAE

~10mm Small, compact moths with a wingspan of up to ~15mm. At rest they appear to be rotund, furry bundles. Wings are grey and white (sometimes brown), red or orange with variable patterns depending on the species. Legs also very thick and furry and are held close to the body at rest. Males have elaborate, comb-like antennae.

HABITS & HABITAT Slug moths are named for their striking caterpillars, which are among the most colourful of all moth larvae and have elaborate spikes. They are very poisonous and should never be handled. Common and widespread in the rainy season.

Green slug moths LIMACODIDAE

15–35mm Robust, medium-sized moths. Their bodies are typically brownish and very furry with thick, dense hairs; they sometimes appear untidy. The wings are marked with variable patches of beautiful soft green and the legs are thick, furry and contrasting.

HABITS & HABITAT Among the most striking of East African moths. Adults are most often seen at the beginning of the rains, when they are attracted to lights and land on walls, or are found perched on leaves or trunks. If bothered, they will bristle slightly and curve the abdomen up. Occur seasonally in forests, woodlands and other moist habitats.

Horn moths TINEIDAE

10–25mm Size and shape variable, but adults are typically narrow-winged, dull moths. Caterpillars are distinctive for the tubular cases (shown here) that they construct on the horns of dead mammals. The pupae often stick out of these rough, wrinkly tubes.

HABITS & HABITAT The horn moth *Ceratophaga vastella* is typically seen on the horns of wildebeest, hartebeest, cattle and impala skulls in the bush. The clothes moths that damage fabrics, carpets and other household materials are closely related. The caterpillars digest the proteins in horns and manufactured items.

Pearl moths CRAMBIDAE

~20mm Elegant, medium-sized moths with a wingspan of 20–30mm. At rest the forewings and hind wings overlap partly, frequently leaving the abdomen visible. Colour varies from pearly white to pale yellow, often with bold stripes and patterns. Their wings are very delicate, often translucent, and are easily damaged if handled or touched.

HABITS & HABITAT These beautiful moths are attracted to lights and may be noticed when they land on walls or tables. Frequently found resting on leaves in forest and wooded areas. Diverse; a few species are pests and some have semi-aquatic larvae.

Green pearl moths *Parotis* spp.

~15mm Elegant moths with a wingspan of 20–30mm. Their wings are a beautiful, fairly uniform, pale, almost translucent green. The head has a short, pointed snout. They have long, often striped, legs and fine antennae. Their eyes are usually darker and contrasting.

HABITS & HABITAT Common and widespread moths in many different kinds of habitat. Can be confused with emeralds (Geometridae), but hold their wings slightly higher and folded down, rather than flat and spread out. The larvae of many species are leaf miners, feeding inside leaves.

Mottled pearl moths *Leucinodes* spp.

~15mm Elegant, medium sized moths with a wingspan of 20–25mm. A recognisable group of moths with very detailed patterns on the wings and a habit of perching with the abdomen curled upwards. At rest, they hold out their long, fine white-and-brown or white-and-black banded forelegs at an angle to the rest of the legs.

HABITS & HABITAT Common and widespread in most habitat types (and seasonally in drylands and arid areas). Most often noticed when they are attracted to lights and land on walls. These very delicate moths breed on *Solanum* and morning glories.

Ermine tent moths *Yponomeuta* spp.

~12mm Wingspan is ~20mm. At rest these moths are unmistakable because of their extremely narrow build and elongate outline. Wings are dull silvery grey with spotting and speckles. The grub-like, gregarious caterpillars construct huge, sheet-like tents of silk on the trees where they feed (main image).

HABITS & HABITAT These seasonal insects are most often noticed when they cover entire trees with silken sheets as they defoliate them. In East Africa, they are most commonly noticed on *Elaeodendron* trees a few weeks after the rains begin.

M N MUTISO

Plume moths PTEROPHORIDAE

~10mm Small moths with a wingspan of 10–15mm. They are ornate, complex and look extremely fragile. A distinctive feature is the marked division of the wings; they also have long, striking, spiny legs.

HABITS & HABITAT A widespread, common and very diverse group of moths present in many different habitats, including drylands. Plume moth caterpillars feed on members of the daisy family (Asteraceae). Most often noticed when perched on grasses, flowers or herbs. They often remain quite still for long periods.

Oblique peacocks GEOMETRIDAE

25–25mm Wingspan of moths at rest is ~30mm. These pale brown, highly variable moths have fine speckling and darker lines cutting across their wings. The edges of the wings have distinct, bluntly angled points.

HABITS & HABITAT A common and widespread group. The caterpillars are the classic 'inchworms' that give rise to the family name Geometridae, meaning 'earth measurers'. Adult moths have a unique and bizarre habit of approaching cattle at night to suck fluid from their eyes!

Scallop moths GEOMETRIDAE

~25mm Common moths with a wingspan of 25–35mm. Colour and patterning are highly variable, both within and between species. Most East African species are pale yellow or yellow-brown with mottling or speckling in various colours. The wings are broad, with scalloped edges.

HABITS & HABITAT Common and widespread in a range of habitats including gardens, woodland and forest areas. Caterpillars feed on a number of different trees, including *Zizyphus* spp. Often seen perched on walls near lights during the rainy season.

Duster moths *Pingasa* spp.

~30mm These moths have a wingspan of 35–40mm. They are highly recognisable, though variable. Their wings are generally pale with incredibly fine, beautiful speckling and spots. When resting on leaves or walls they hold their wings flat, with a slight space between the forewings and hind wings.

HABITS & HABITAT Among the most common moths, especially at the beginning of the rains, when they can be found on walls near lights at night, or resting on foliage or tree trunks during the day. They inhabit gardens, woodland, forest and moist habitats.

Mottled Victoria *Victoria* spp.

~15mm Moths with a wingspan of 20–25mm. Wings are a soft pale green with white spots and fine white speckling. Patterning varies, but is always very intricate and lace-like. Among the most beautiful of geometrid moths.

HABITS & HABITAT Superbly camouflaged, these amazing moths simply 'melt' away when resting on lichen-covered trunks and branches during the day. Seen mostly at night, when they are drawn to lights and land on walls. In East Africa they occur in forests, woodland and gardens in moist habitats.

Emeralds GEOMETRINAE

10–15mm Wingspan varies depending on the species, but is typically 15–25mm. A very familiar and recognisable groups of moths. Adult moths are an almost uniform, soft pale green. Some species have yellow or white edging to the wings. Occasionally the wings are marked with a dark or light spot or fine speckling.

HABITS & HABITAT One of the most common, widespread and ubiquitous groups of moths and found in virtually all habitat types, including arid areas during the rainy season. The caterpillars exploit a wide range of plants for food, including several cultivated species.

Wisp wing moths GEOMETRIDAE

10–15mm Also known as 'thorn moths' or 'ragged thorns'. A number of different species have this irregular, raised wing shape. Their most distinctive feature is seen when the moths are at rest: the forewings and hind wings are clearly separated. The forewings are held up and rolled or folded; in many species this provides superb camouflage.

HABITS & HABITAT Fairly common and widespread in bush, savanna, riverine forest and woodland areas. When perched on thorny bushes can seem to disappear as they mimic the vegetation remarkably well.

Barred carpet moths *Xanthorhoe spp.*

~10mm Small moths with a wingspan of 10–12mm. Dark with speckled patterns, which provide perfect camouflage when these moths rest during the day on moss- or lichen-covered tree trunks. Fairly stocky, with fat abdomens. Colour and patterning vary depending on the species.

HABITS & HABITAT A widespread and very common group of moths. Familiar to gardeners and farmers, as the caterpillars are pests of a number of cultivated plants, including carrots and lettuce. Found in most habitat types.

Small wild silk moths   BOMBYCIDAE

15–20mm Usually medium-sized moths with a variable wingspan (20–35mm). The shape and posture of the adult moths are distinctive: they have stocky bodies with narrow wings, held closely together and raised when at rest. Typically cream to brownish in colour, with feathery antennae and short, furry legs.
HABITS & HABITAT These common and widespread moths are most often seen as adults, when they are attracted to lights. The adult moths raise their abdomens, twitch and drop to the ground if touched or disturbed. Caterpillars feed on a range of plants including figs and mulberries (family Moraceae).

Gonometa silk moths   *Gonometa* spp.

30–55mm A group of large, robust, wild silk moths with a wingspan of 50–95mm. At rest, the long, elegant forewings are held close to the body. Adult moths, like *G. nysa* shown here, are brown to red-brown, but variable (top). Caterpillars are massive and covered with irritating hairs, as in *Gonometa podocarpi* (bottom).
HABITS & HABITAT Fairly common and widespread in habitats from bush to forest. Moths are often seen at lights, where they react by playing dead if touched. The silk with which the caterpillars spin their cocoons could potentially be a source of silk for human use.

Lunar moth   *Argema mimosae*

M.N. MUTISO

~200mm Among the most beautiful of African moths. Large, elegant and unmistakable, with a wingspan of 120–150mm. The forewings are pale yellow-green with small striking eyespots and are edged in red-brown and ochre. The hind wings also have eyespots (hidden by forewings in this photograph) and long, elegant tails. Caterpillars are massive bright green insects with blue-and-yellow bands and bold spines.
HABITS & HABITAT A moth of warm woodland and forest regions, including coastal bush and forest. Adult moths are often seen when drawn to lights. The caterpillar spins a silvery cocoon.

Cabbage tree emperor
Bunaea spp.

40–50mm Large, striking moths with a wingspan of ~160mm. Adult moths are brown with pretty speckling, prominent eyespots on the hind wings and variable patterning. Unmistakable caterpillars (shown here) are more often noticed than the adult moths themselves: they are large, jet-black with red-and-yellow spines.

HABITS & HABITAT Common and widespread seasonally in savanna, woodland and moist habitats. Caterpillars are often noticed feeding in numbers on trees, including *Balanites, Croton, Cussonia* and others. The adults are often drawn to lights.

White-ringed atlas
Epiphora spp.

60mm Large moths with a wingspan of 80–100mm. Beautiful, elegant and striking with large forewings that have expanded, curved wing tips. Hind and forewings are grey, with clear central eyespots and elegant white lines and speckling in many different hues. The body is stout and hairy. They have feathery antennae.

HABITS & HABITAT Fairly common and widespread in riverine, bush, woodland and forest habitats. Often drawn to lights, where they flap about clumsily; also found perched on leaves in forested areas during the rains.

Yellow emperor moths
SATURNIIDAE

40–50mm Striking and noticeable emperor moths with a wingspan of 150–200mm. There are several similar, related species. Adult moths are robust, stocky, with beautiful, mostly pale yellow or ochre-yellow wings with variable eyespots, and other fine markings.

HABITS & HABITAT Seasonally among the most commonly encountered emperor moths in East Africa. Found in a range of vegetation from bush to forest. In adults flight is clumsy and bumbling. Caterpillars are large and black with green-yellow speckling.

Convolvulus hawkmoth — *Agrius convolvuli*

50–60mm Large, elegant hawkmoths with a
wingspan of 90–110mm. Perhaps the best known
of all hawkmoths. Adults are pale grey with
finely speckled and lined wings. The abdomen
(often hidden at rest) is striking with contrasting
alternating pink and black bands. Eyes large and
dark. The proboscis is long and flexible.

HABITS & HABITAT Common and widespread
across a wide range of habitats from bush to
forest. Often seen visiting flowers at dusk,
including *Turraea,* honeysuckle, jasmine
(*Jasminium*), pyjama lilies (*Crinum*) and orchids.
Frequently drawn to lights at night.

Fulvous hawkmoth — *Coelonia fulvinotata*

50–60mm Large, with a wingspan of 100–110mm.
These well-built moths have heavy bodies and
powerful wings. The forewings are mostly brown
and finely patterned; the hind wings are yellow
and brown. Their bodies are brown with bands
and have small pink-and-black central patches.
They have a long, flexible proboscis.

HABITS & HABITAT Common and widespread
in forest and woodland, including gallery forest
in riverine areas. Adults may be seen visiting
flowers with long tubes, including many plants
specifically adapted for pollination by means of a
long tongue. These are well-known examples of
co-evolution between plants and their pollinators.

Comma hawkmoths — *Nephele* spp.

40–45mm Stocky moths with a wingspan of
~75mm. Robust, with very strong wings and thick
bodies. Wings are variable: greenish to brownish,
with green or blackish tints and patterns. There is
a distinctive, comma-shaped, silver-white marking
in the middle of each forewing. Eyes are large and
dark. Proboscis measures ~40mm.

HABITS & HABITAT Very common and
widespread moths that can be found visiting
flowers at dusk in habitats from bush to forest.
They fly fast and dextrously, moving methodically
between flowers. They are important pollinators
of flowers with medium-sized floral tubes,
including cultivated papaya (pawpaws).

White-barred hawk *Leucostrophus hirundo*

~20mm A small, common and familiar hawkmoth with a wingspan of ~25mm. Body striking with contrasting black and white bands; resembles a carpenter bee when in flight. The wings are pale grey-brown. Proboscis is short, but flexible.

HABITS & HABITAT Often seen visiting flowers in bush, savanna, woodland and grassland areas. Easily mistaken for a carpenter bee, as it moves swiftly and nervously between flowers. Hovers while feeding on nectar using its proboscis.

Oriental bee hawk *Cephonodes hylas*

~30mm A medium-sized, striking hawkmoth with a wingspan of 40–45mm. Body is variable pastel yellow-green with red-brown background colouring. The black tail is fanned out in flight. The legs and belly are whitish and the wings clear, with veins neatly outlined in black. Eyes large and dark. Has a relatively long proboscis.

HABITS & HABITAT Seasonally common and widespread in many different habitats. Flight active and powerful, moving between flowers during the day. While hovering and feeding it resembles a large, noisy bee. Has a worldwide distribution.

Verdant hawkmoths *Basiothia* spp.

~25mm Small, striking and recognisable hawkmoths with a wingspan of 35–40mm. Bodies are robust and elegant with powerful, streamlined wings. Body and forewings are a beautiful soft, pale green and the hind wings are a contrasting orange. Has flexible proboscis and mottled eyes.

HABITS & HABITAT Common and widespread in most habitats seasonally, especially in bush and savanna areas. Often seen visiting flowers in the early evening, including jasmine, *Pentanisia* and mass-flowering trees and shrubs. Frequently seen at lights.

Silver-striped hawkmoth *Hippotion celerio*

~45mm Medium-sized moths with a wingspan of ~65mm. They are elegant with a robust, but very streamlined body and powerful, pointed wings. Body pale tan with variable white markings. Forewings tan with beautiful silver-white stripes; hind wings pink to red. The eyes are large and dark, while the proboscis is long and flexible for taking nectar.

HABITS & HABITAT Among the most common and widespread hawkmoths. Active at dusk, in the early morning and at the beginning of the rains. Often seen at flowers during the day. They visit a wide range of flowers, avidly drinking nectar.

Lappet moths LASIOCAMPIDAE

15–45mm Small to medium-sized, highly variable moths. They are stocky and robust, with very hairy bodies. At rest they appear densely furry, often with tufts of protruding fur. The forewings are narrower than the hind wings. Colour varies, often providing good camouflage.

HABITS & HABITAT These moths are most often seen when resting on tree trunks, where they can be incredibly well hidden. They are drawn to lights, and are often found on walls or tents where they remain still for long periods. Found primarily in forest, woodland and moist bush; some species also occur in gardens.

Processionary moths THAUMETOPOIEDAE

15–25mm A variable group of moths with a wingspan of 20–45mm. Adults are beautiful and robust, with broad, triangular wings folded back over the body at rest. Usually pale with darker brown or red-brown stripes (inset).

HABITS & HABITAT Found in forest and woodland areas in East Africa. Adults are often drawn to lights. Named for the caterpillars' habit of walking in lines. Caterpillars are often found in masses on the trunks of trees (main image). They are hairy and can cause irritation if handled. Pupation also occurs en masse.

Beautiful tiger moths
Amphicallia spp.

~35mm Fairly large, striking and easily recognised moths with a wingspan of 60–65mm. Their wings are bright orange, striped with slightly irregular, bold black bands that have a dusting of blue at their centres. The head is small, with black eyes and fine antennae.
HABITS & HABITAT Fairly common moths encountered during the rainy season in areas of moist bush, woodland and forest, including highland forest areas. The caterpillars have black and white stripes, are often found perched on vegetation during the day and feed on *Crotolaria* and other legumes.

Orange tiger moths
Secusio spp.

~22mm Medium-sized, elegant tiger moths with a wingspan of ~35mm. They rest with their wings folded back and have pale orange hind wings (visible in flight, but hidden at rest) and brown forewings. There is a broken white stripe across the middle of each forewing. Head is small, with fine antennae.
HABITS & HABITAT Common and widespread in many habitats from bush to woodland areas. Often found perched on flowers, especially at the beginning of the rains. As the moth alights, the orange hind wings are tucked away, causing it to 'vanish'.

Stocky tiger moths
Balacra spp.

~35mm Fairly large, stocky, very striking moths with a wingspan of 40–50mm. They have pale yellow-white wings with veins outlined in black. The body is fat, the head and thorax are boldly patterned with thick orange tufts of fur, and the abdomen is long and brightly banded with short red stripes on a white background.
HABITS & HABITAT Fairly common moths in moist woodland and forest in the western parts of the region. Often drawn to lights at night, where they perch on walls and can be found still resting during the day. If touched or handled they often feign death, barely moving.

Frother tiger moths
Amerila spp.

~30mm Medium-sized moths with a wingspan of 45–50mm. Beautiful, elegant and easily recognised. At rest the wings are folded neatly over the body, concealing the abdomen and giving a pear-shaped outline. Wings are pale yellow with translucent windows. The thorax is spotted, and the eyes and legs are orange. The bright orange abdomen is concealed at rest, but visible in flight or when alarmed.

HABITS & HABITAT Common and widespread in East Africa. Name 'frother' refers to their defensive behaviour – they produce toxic bubbly liquid when bothered or touched.

White frothers
Amerila spp.

~30mm Medium-sized moths with a wingspan of 45–50mm. Stunning, almost dazzling, white moths with diaphanous wings. Both forewings and hind wings are translucent white, with slightly outlined veins. Head and thorax have variable black or orange spotting. The eyes are small and black. Legs often brightly coloured. In many species the abdomen is yellow or red and is flashed as a warning signal when the moth is alarmed.

HABITS & HABITAT Among the more common and widespread moths in East Africa. Found in moist bush and forest areas. They secrete frothy toxins and squeak if roughly handled.

Speckled footman moths
Utethesia spp.

~20mm A small, narrow, very recognisable moth with a wingspan of 25–30mm. At rest, the wings are folded neatly over the body, giving it a narrow, elegant outline. The forewings are white, speckled with black (and some red) spots. The hind wings are black-and-white, with bold black-and-red patterns. Head is small, with black eyes.

HABITS & HABITAT One of the most widely distributed moths in the world. Ubiquitous in most habitats. Often seen during the day as it flies with a weak fluttering motion. Feeds on a wide range of plants, including some crops and garden plants.

Plated footman moths *Sozusa* spp.

20–25mm A medium-sized moth with a wingspan of 30–35mm. Slender, elegant, with a narrow, almost cylindrical appearance when at rest. The wings are a dull grey with variable pale orange markings and a slight metallic sheen. Head is small and is kept tucked in. Legs, head and antennae are often pale orange.

HABITS & HABITAT Common and widespread in a wide range of habitats from bush to forest. Often attracted to lights and can be found resting on walls or tents. Flight nervous and fluttering. If handled, produces toxic liquids in self-defence.

Ghost moths (ethereals) LYMANTRIIDAE

20–25mm Stocky, medium-sized moths with a wingspan of ~30mm. A highly variable group. Adults are typically white or pale yellow, with diaphanous, slightly translucent wings and stocky, very hairy, often untidy bodies.

HABITS & HABITAT Very common and widespread in woodland, forest, gardens and other moist habitats. Often found at lights at night or perching on vegetation during the day. Many similar, related species occur. *Olapa* spp. (shown here) are often seen on leaves during the day. They are reluctant to move and easily shed their thick hairs if bothered.

Fig tree moths *Naroma* spp.

12–15mm Small moths with a wingspan of ~20mm. Unusual, very compact, robust and easily recognised. At rest the wings are tucked close to the body, giving a triangular, tent-like form. The fat, furry thorax and thick, hairy legs are also distinctive. They are pale ivory with variable faint markings.

HABITS & HABITAT Common and widespread in woodland, forest and riverine areas where their host food plants, fig trees (*Ficus* spp.), grow. Adult moths are often found perched on leaves during the day. Also drawn to lights. They tend to hunker down and tuck in their legs, playing dead if bothered, and are reluctant to fly away. Flight is clumsy and slow.

Banded tussock moths
LYMANTRIIDAE

20–30mm Medium-sized moths with a wingspan of 30–40mm. A highly variable and diverse group. Adult moths (main image) are generally white or pale yellow, with variable dark speckling or stripes on their wings. Bodies are fat and very furry. Legs are thick and covered with very long, somewhat untidy hairs that are very noticeable at rest.
HABITS & HABITAT Common and widespread moths, found on the edges of forests and in woodland and moist bush. Drawn to lights. Often found perched on walls, windows and tents at the beginning of the rains. They curl up the abdomen when alarmed, which allows for the long hairs to detach into the face or mouth of a would-be predator.

Bollworm moths
NOCTUIDAE

~10mm Small moths with a wingspan of 15–20mm. Bollworm moths are a widespread and variable group. At rest, their wings are folded down, which gives the body a sharp, triangular outline. The forewings are yellow-green, with variable rusty markings or tinted edges. The hind wings are pale or white.
HABITS & HABITAT Common and widespread moths in many different habitats including gardens and cultivated areas. The caterpillars are spiny and feed on the buds of crops as well as inside young cotton bolls. Adults are often found perched on leaves or stems.

Silver U-moths
Chrysodeixes spp.

~12mm Medium-sized moths with a wingspan of 30–35mm. Adult moths are distinguished by their irregular outline and tufts of fur on the thorax. Brown, with variable darker patches and fine lines. Each forewing bears an obvious silver-white U-shaped marking and a spot. Legs thick and hairy. Head is smallish with fine antennae.
HABITS & HABITAT Common and ubiquitous moths across the region. The caterpillars can be serious pests in gardens and on farms, feeding on the leaves and shoots of canna lilies, bananas and potatoes. They are related to the infamous armyworms (*Spodoptera*).

Beer (sundowner) moth
Sphingomorpha chlorea

~40mm Large, robust, familiar moths with a
wingspan of 55–60mm. Rather dull, but fluffy.
They have strong brown forewings with fine
bands and patterns, and paler hind wings. The
thorax is dark with a central stripe. Legs are long
with furry bases and the eyes often glow red.
They have long, fine antennae.

HABITS & HABITAT Attracted to ripening fruit
and alcohol and often fall into people's drinks. They
puncture ripe fruit with the proboscis. Caterpillars
occur on many plants, including acacias.

Walker's owl moth
Erebus macrops

~60mm Very large moths, with a wingspan of
~120mm. They have brown wings covered in
gorgeous, fine, dark patterns. Each forewing has
a prominent dark red and bluish eyespot. The
hind wings are a darker chocolate brown with
dark brown bars. Head is small, with tiny black
eyes. They have fine, narrow antennae.

HABITS & HABITAT Common and widespread.
When flushed, may be seen fluttering and
coming to rest a short distance away. Frequently
rest in the eaves of roofs, buttresses of trees or
on the sheltered sides of buildings. Adults are
often attracted to lights at night. The caterpillars
are large and feed on *Entada* trees.

Fruit-piercer moths (underwings)
Eudocima spp.

~40mm Large and conspicuous with a wingspan
of 90–100mm. Highly recognisable. They have
beautiful forewings, with finely barred markings
and white lines. The hind wings are a very
striking bright orange with variable black edging
or spots. The thorax is pale brown and fat, and
the head is small, with fine antennae.

HABITS & HABITAT Common and widespread
in areas of moist bush, woodland and forest, as
well as in cultivated areas. Adults can be pests,
as they pierce and slightly damage ripe fruit.
At rest the orange wings are hidden, but are
startlingly revealed if the moth is disturbed and
flies away.

Red-tail moths
Enmonodia spp.

~35mm Large, robust moths with a wingspan of
50–55mm. The elegant, broad wings have pointed,
streamlined edges. Wings are brown-grey with
variable fine darker stripes and speckling. The
abdomen is a bright contrasting orange-red. The
head is small, with tiny eyes and fine antennae.

HABITS & HABITAT Fairly common moths that
are often flushed by people walking in woodland
or forest. They flutter away, coming to rest
among leaves or in sheltered spots. Orange-red
colouring is flashed in flight, then 'disappears'
as the moth lands.

Achaea moth caterpillars
Achaea spp.

20–50mm A widespread group of caterpillars
whose members change size, shape and colour
as they develop. Early-stage caterpillars are
mostly soft black; older caterpillars become
more colourful and are striped and speckled in
browns and reds, with pale spots. They have
enlarged, bulbous heads.

HABITS & HABITAT They are widely recognised,
often gregarious, feeding in large numbers
on leaves. Highly seasonal, but with irregular
outbreaks in forested areas across Africa, when
they may defoliate trees. Can be seen dropping
down from the canopy in large numbers on
untidy silk threads.

Achaea moths
Achaea spp.

~30mm Large, robust moths with a wingspan
of 45–50mm. There are many similar, closely
related species. They are stocky, well built, with
greyish-brown forewings that have variable fine
markings. The hind wings are usually darker,
with variable blackish patches and white spots.
They have smallish heads with fine antennae
and a short, flexible proboscis.

HABITS & HABITAT Among the most common
and widespread moths in East Africa, found from
rainforest areas to semi-desert (where they occur
seasonally following rains). They often enter camps
and buildings, attracted to the lights. They flutter
noisily and often present in noticeable numbers in
forested areas, especially in dry weather.

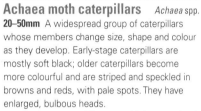

M.N. MUTISO

One-pip policeman
Coeliades anchises

~30mm Robust butterflies with a wingspan of 40–45mm. They have strong, elegant wings. The forewings are long and pointed, while the hind wings have a broad white band on their undersides, readily visible at rest. The distinguishing feature of this species is a single black spot on the underside of each hind wing.

HABITS & HABITAT Widely distributed in forest, woodland and savanna habitats of East Africa. Their flight is fast and they tend to whizz by at great speeds, pausing to rest on leaves or flowers. They frequent damp patches to sip salts and regularly visit flowers.

Spotless policeman
Coeliades forestan

~30mm A robust butterfly with a wingspan of 40–45mm. The wings are strong, beautifully shaped and very streamlined. Brown, with a broad white stripe that is clearly visible on the undersides of the wings when the butterfly is at rest. However, there is no black spot on the wings in this species. Each antenna forms a tapering club at its tip. Has a thick body, with tufts of orange fur that are also found on the legs.

HABITS & HABITAT Very widely distributed from bush to forest areas. Flight is fast and somewhat erratic; often moves very rapidly between patches of flowers. Occasionally pauses to rest on leaves. Caterpillars feed on many different plants.

Elfins
Sarangesa spp.

~20mm Small, compact skippers with a wingspan of 30–35mm. There are many closely related species, all with similar colouring and patterns. Wings are variable shades of brown, with darker markings, splotches and translucent windows. Eyes are bright and blackish.

HABITS & HABITAT Among the most common and widespread of African butterflies. Typical of open habitats, from grassland to more arid habitats, appearing after the rains. They fly low, with fast, fluttering movements, frequently resting on grasses, leaves or stones. Often found roosting in outhouses, on walls, in animal burrows and on termite mounds.

Grizzled skippers

Spialia spp.

~10mm Small, dainty butterflies with a wingspan of ~15mm. Their beautiful blackish wings are covered in variable bright white, ivory or pale yellow spots. Their bodies are fairly robust, with striped abdomens. They have stout, clubbed antennae.

HABITS & HABITAT A common and widespread group of butterflies whose members are seasonally common in drylands. Flight is fast and very erratic, making these butterflies difficult to follow with the eye. They rest with wings held open, and eat a wide range of food plants from several different families.

Swift skippers

Borbo spp.

15–20mm Medium-sized with a wingspan of 25–30mm. The forewings are fairly elongate relative to the hind wings, with a variable series of semi-translucent or white spots. Both body and wings are typically soft darkish brown, with hints of ochre-yellow in some species. Antennae are tapered clubs, the eyes are dark and the abdomen is short.

HABITS & HABITAT Typically rest with the hind wings splayed out and the forewings folded back in the characteristic fashion of skippers. Primarily grassland butterflies, but some species occur in arid areas. Caterpillars feed on various species of grasses.

Buff-tipped skippers

Netrobalane spp.

~20mm Medium-sized butterflies with a wingspan of ~30mm. Beautiful and distinctive, with creamish-white wings that have intricate markings, resembling faded ancient writing, and warm buff-coloured wing tips. Wing edges have an irregular outline. The legs, antennae and proboscis are prominent and strong.

HABITS & HABITAT Fairly common and widespread across East Africa, often in savanna or woodland. Males are territorial and will patrol and defend a patch of suitable habitat. Often seen visiting flowers and sipping salts from damp patches.

Hottentot skippers
Gegenes spp.

~12mm Small skippers with a wingspan of
20–25mm. The forewings are narrow and
elegant, with slightly pointed tips; the hind
wings are short and rounded. Colour varies, but
typically a soft shade of brown to ochre-yellow.
The undersides of the wings are more yellow
than the upper sides. These skippers have dark
eyes and relatively long, tapered antennae.
HABITS & HABITAT Among the most common
and widely distributed butterflies of the region.
Found seasonally both at high altitudes and in
drylands. Flight is fast and erratic; they pause
often to sip nectar and bask in the sun.

Orange sprite
Celaenorrhinus spp.

~25mm A medium-sized, pretty and active
butterfly with a wingspan of ~35mm. Wings are
dark brown, marked with variable yellow-orange
spots and fine speckling. The body is thick
and rather furry, with long antennae that have
tapered, club-shaped tips.
HABITS & HABITAT A common and widespread
forest butterfly that is often found flying in small
glades and along roads. Stops frequently to
sun itself on foliage, and rests with the wings
spread out flat. Frequently visits flowers for
nectar. The caterpillars feed on forest herbs,
including *Justicia* and *Hypoestes*.

Orange-spotted skipper
Zenonia zeno

~15mm A medium-sized butterfly with a
compact and elegant body. The wings are dark
brown with bright orange spots and markings
and the forewings are longer than the hind
wings. Like many skippers, rests with the
hind wings held separate, angled away from
the forewings.
HABITS & HABITAT One of the most common
and charming skipper butterflies in the region.
Found mainly in highland areas near woodland
and forest, but also fairly common in gardens.
Flight is fast and erratic; stops often to bask on
leaves. The caterpillars feed on various species
of grasses, as well as maize and sorghum.

M N MUTISO

Spotted sylph
Asictopterus stellata

~10mm A small skipper with a wingspan of ~25mm. One of the most recognisable skippers in the region. It has an attractive, compact build. The upper surfaces of the wings are black with white spots. The undersides of the wings are a pure ochre-yellow with bold white spots that have black edges.

HABITS & HABITAT A butterfly of coastal woodland and forest in Kenya and Tanzania. Often found flying along forest trails and roads, stopping frequently to sip nectar from low-growing wildflowers. Frequently rests on grasses.

Netted sylphs
Metisella spp.

~15mm Medium-sized skipper butterflies with a wingspan of 30–32mm. They are among the most elegant and unique of East African butterflies. The upper sides of the wings are an almost uniform dark chocolate brown. The undersides are beautifully patterned with a bold, net-like, light yellow and dark brown design.

HABITS & HABITAT Active butterflies found in southern Kenya and Tanzania; often encountered visiting wildflowers in the shade of acacias in grassland and savanna areas. They fly with a slow, fluttering movement, staying in the shade, where they are often found resting.

Pale ranger
Kedestes callicles

~10mm A small, beautiful, compact skipper butterfly with a wingspan of ~20mm. Its most distinctive feature is the net-like pattern of black-bordered creamish-white spots on the undersides of the ochre-yellow wings.

HABITS & HABITAT Found in the savanna of the eastern and central regions, where it tends to keep to the shade, often visiting flowers such as *Plectranthus* and *Orthosiphon*. Flight is low and fluttering. Can be nervous if approached.

African queen (African monarch)
Danaus chrysippus

~50mm Beautiful, elegant, unmistakable butterflies with a wingspan of 65–75mm. The body is black with white spots. They have bold orange wings with black and white spotted tips or edges. Polymorphic, with several forms, in various combinations of black, orange and white.
HABITS & HABITAT Highly recognisable. Seasonally abundant following rains, their flight is characteristically buoyant and sailing. They migrate within the region. Often seen fluttering around flowering milkweeds, where they take nectar and where females lay their eggs. Mimicked by a number of different butterflies. Caterpillars are smooth and boldly striped.

African blue tiger
Tirumala petiverana

~50mm One of the most beautiful and elegant butterflies of East Africa, with a wingspan of 75–80mm. The jet-black wings are patterned with light blue spots and streaks. Its body is black with white spots and it has a flexible black proboscis and black antennae.
HABITS & HABITAT Common and seasonally widespread in a wide range of habitats, from coastal forest and woodland to gallery forest and wetter savanna. Migrates across the region. Males visit wet patches and elephant dung. Mimicked by a number of swallowtail and swordtail species.

Beautiful tiger
Tirumala formosa

~50mm A beautiful, elegant butterfly with a wingspan of 80–85mm; the largest of the tiger butterflies. Wings are dark brownish-black with pale yellow spots, patches and streaks. The base of each forewing has variable chestnut patch.
HABITS & HABITAT A somewhat localised butterfly of highland forest areas, but occasionally seen in gardens too. Flight is slow and elegant. Often found mud-puddling at the edges of streams or roads. Flies up towards the forest canopy if startled. Being toxic (like the African queen), is mimicked by the region's largest butterfly, the regal swallowtail.

Monk butterflies
Amauris spp.

~40mm Large, elegant butterflies with a
wingspan of ~80mm. The jet-black forewings
have variable white spots and patches. Hind
wings are blackish-brown with white areas near
the base of each wing. The body, head and legs
are black.

HABITS & HABITAT They fly gracefully in
forested areas, with a slow, buoyant movement.
Often found sunning themselves on the
ground with wings spread. They participate in
mud-puddling for salts along forest roads and
streams. Can be locally common at some sites
following the rains.

Chief butterflies
Amauris spp.

~40mm Large butterflies with a wingspan of
~80mm. There are a number of closely related,
very similar-looking butterflies that can be difficult
to tell apart. Forewings are black with variable
white spots. Hind wings are blackish-brown with
pale ochre-yellow patches and white spots. Head,
body, legs and antennae are all black.

HABITS & HABITAT They are among the most
common butterflies in highland forest, woodland
and gardens. Often seen at flowers and mud-
puddling in forest areas. At times very large
numbers of these butterflies visit cowpats and
fresh urine on the ground.

Elegant acraea
Acraea perenna

~35mm Gorgeous, large, striking butterflies
with a wingspan of 65–70mm. They have black
bodies, with orange-tipped abdomens. Their
wings are fiery orange red and black. The colour
is so intense that it almost glows in sunlight.

HABITS & HABITAT Fairly abundant, though
localised, butterflies that inhabit forest and
savanna. Often seen visiting flowers and mud-
puddling on the ground. Their flight is slow,
elegant and sailing, but they will fly up into
the canopy if disturbed. They contain toxins
and their bold colouring is a classic example
of warning coloration. A few other butterfly
species mimic them.

Tiny acraea
Acraea uvui

~10mm A small, dainty butterfly with a wingspan of ~20mm. Striking and easily recognised, there are several similar, closely related species. Wings are black with bold, rich orange patches on forewings and hind wings, which align when the butterfly is at rest.
HABITS & HABITAT A common and widespread species often found gathered in large numbers at animal dung or visiting flowers. Typically found in highland forest habitats and can be very abundant. Tiny acraeas sometimes cluster together when feeding.

Dancing acraea
Acraea eponina

~12mm Colourful, medium-sized butterflies with a wingspan of 15–20mm. Wings are a rich, bright orange with variable, comma-shaped black markings on each forewing; both forewings and hind wings have black edging. Antennae are black and the eyes have white spots. Abdomen has beautiful black-and-orange patterns.
HABITS & HABITAT Among East Africa's prettiest butterflies. Found in a wide range of habitats but most abundant in savanna and moist bush. Often found visiting flowers, where they sit for long periods, gently opening and closing their wings. Caterpillars feed on plants in the genera *Hibiscus, Sterculia* and *Triumfetta*.

Dusky acraea
Acraea esebria

~20mm A medium-sized butterfly with a wingspan of ~40mm. One of the most variable butterflies in the acraea group. Colour ranges from yellow to orange, with some white patches. Head and thorax have white spots, and abdomen is neatly spotted with pale orange dots.
HABITS & HABITAT A common and widespread butterfly in forest, woodland and even agricultural areas. Often found perched on flowers, where it sips nectar. The caterpillars develop on stinging nettles (Urticaceae).

Encedon acraea *Acraea encedon*

~15mm A medium-sized, very common and
variable butterfly with a wingspan of ~40mm.
Wings can be off-white or yellow to pale orange-
brown; they are marked with greyish-black lines,
dots and patterns. The edges of the wings are
outlined in black. Abdomen is rich ochre-yellow
with a black stripe down its centre.

HABITS & HABITAT One of the most abundant
butterflies of grassland, bush and savanna
regions. Often found in gardens visiting
flowering weeds. Interestingly, the sex ratio is
highly biased towards females because of what
is thought to be infection with a male-killing
bacterial parasite. Often found roosting in large
numbers. Engages in hill-topping on sunny days.

Clear-winged acraea *Acraea semivitrea*

~20mm A beautiful and distinctive insect with a
wingspan of ~40mm. Elegant wings with large,
clear 'windows' make this species unmistakable.
Forewings are mostly clear, with the veins
outlined in black. Hind wings are mostly black
with a pale yellow band on the inner edge and
have clear 'window' from the middle towards the
outer edge. Lower abdomen is also pale yellow.

HABITS & HABITAT A fairly common rainforest
butterfly. Clear-winged acraeas fly high up in the
canopy but are often found sunning themselves
on roads or visiting damp patches, dung or carrion.
Very striking when basking on leaves or the
ground with the light passing through their wings.

Polka dot *Pardopsis punctatissima*

~15mm A tiny, dainty butterfly with a wingspan
of ~30mm. As the name suggests, this is
a distinctive butterfly: the orange-brown
forewings and hind wings are covered in neatly
distributed dots. The thorax and abdomen are
pale orange with a variable central black stripe.

HABITS & HABITAT A widespread species
found seasonally in grassland, savanna and arid
areas. Flies low and very weakly, fluttering and
pausing frequently to rest on stems. Sometimes
present in very large numbers following rains.

Eyed ringlets
Neocoenyra spp.

~20mm Dainty, medium-sized butterflies with a wingspan of 15–20mm. The body is thin and dark. Wings are rich sepia brown with variable orange-brown patches near the tips of the forewings. Bold eyespots occur on both forewings and hind wings (but tend to be larger on forewings). They have small eyes and fine antennae.

HABITS & HABITAT Common and widespread in grassland and savanna as well as woodland glades across the region. Often seen sunning themselves in half-shade, slowly and gently opening and closing their wings. Caterpillars feed on grasses.

Bush browns
Bicyclus spp.

~25mm A fairly large, robust butterfly with a wingspan of ~50mm. Highly recognisable, yet variable, with many similar, closely related species. The large eyespot on the underside of each forewing is diagnostic (but sometimes hidden when wings are folded). Edges of hind wings are wavy.

HABITS & HABITAT Browns are among the most common groups of butterflies in a wide range of habitats. Some of the forest-dwelling species can be endemic. The most widespread is *Bicyclus safitza* (shown here), which has become an important laboratory insect in studies of the genetics underlying the development of eyespots and other features.

Banded evening brown
Gnophodes betsimena

~35mm A large, robust, highly variable butterfly with a wingspan of 55–60mm. The wings are broad, with irregular margins. Colour ranges from pale grey-brown to chocolate brown, with varied stripes and speckling. Resembles a dry leaf.

HABITS & HABITAT A widespread and common butterfly in highland woodland and forest areas. Rests during the day among the leaf litter and flies up abruptly when startled, quickly coming to rest a short distance away. At rest, almost invisible against the forest floor. Caterpillars feed on forest grasses.

E.M. GITONGA

African emigrant
Catopsilia florella

~40mm Large butterflies with a wingspan of 55–60mm. One of the most familiar butterflies of the region. Sleek, elegant and powerful. Males are a beautiful greenish-white, while females are more variable – from dull white to yellow.
HABITS & HABITAT A fast butterfly that flies swiftly between flowers. Often engages in mud-puddling, sometimes in large numbers with other butterflies. There are periodic movements of these butterflies across Africa. Caterpillars feed on *Sesbania* and *Cassia*, often attended by ants.

M.N. MUTSO

Vagrants
Nepheronia spp.

~40mm Large butterflies with a wingspan of 55–60mm. One of the most striking groups of white butterflies in East Africa. Wings are large, broad and white, with hints of blue or a green sheen. The wings are tipped with a black band of variable width. Females often have small orange patches at the bases of their wings.
HABITS & HABITAT One of the fastest butterflies, flying swiftly and sleekly through the air. Fairly nervous; will often fly away if approached. Frequently visits flowers, especially in dryland areas. Various species have specialised for particular habitats, ranging from forest to semi-desert areas.

Brown-veined white
Belenois aurota

~25mm Medium-sized, familiar and widespread butterflies with a wingspan of 40–45mm. They have beautiful white wings with veins outlined in dark brown. The intensity of brown varies, and is sometimes very faded. Eyes are bright and mottled.
HABITS & HABITAT Among the most familiar butterflies of East Africa, brown-veined whites have a tendency to migrate en masse, often passing right through cities in very large numbers. When they have increased locally and defoliated the plants that their caterpillars (inset) feed on, they search for new areas in which to lay eggs.

Dotted borders
Mylothris spp.

~35mm Fairly large, common and familiar butterflies with a wingspan of ~50mm. Wings are a soft white with variable orange patches and yellowish tints on the undersides or wing bases. The edges of the wings have a series of black spots, which vary in size and shape.
HABITS & HABITAT Very common in parks, gardens, woodland and forest areas where they can be seen fluttering lazily in the sunshine. They often settle on leaves to sun themselves, and males participate in mud-puddling during the hottest times of day.

Zebra white
Pinacopteryx eriphia

~25mm A medium-sized, distinctive butterfly with a wingspan of ~40mm. The upper sides of the wings are boldly patterned in soft black and creamish-white. The undersides are brownish and cream with an orange mark at the base of each wing.
HABITS & HABITAT Widely distributed in grassland and savanna areas during the rainy season. These active butterflies move frequently, visiting flowers for nectar; they are especially fond of *Gutenbergia*, *Vernonia* and related species. At rest on the ground or in dry grass, with wings folded, these butterflies are well camouflaged, and resemble leaves.

Grass yellows
Eurema spp.

15–20mm Small, compact, pretty butterflies with a wingspan of 25–30mm. Their bright yellow black-edged wings are easily recognised. A number of closely related, similar-looking species occur in the region.
HABITS & HABITAT Abundant and ubiquitous in bush, grassland and savanna habitats. They can be especially numerous after rains, when large numbers gather at damp spots on roadsides, at puddles, at pools of urine or at streams. The caterpillars eat a wide range of plants, including many legumes.

African golden Arab
Colotis aurigeneus

~25mm A beautiful, medium-sized butterfly with a wingspan of ~40mm. The rich golden-yellow wings are marked with black spots and veins. The base of each wing has a small white patch. Their undersides are more muted, and the eyes are mottled grey.

HABITS & HABITAT A common and widespread butterfly found in a wide range of habitats including savanna, grassland and semi-desert areas after good rains. Also found in higher-altitude grassland. Active butterflies, they flutter about, often stopping at wildflowers for nectar.

Yellow splendour
Colotis protomedia

~40mm Large, striking, elegant butterflies with a wingspan of ~55mm. The wings are a rich pale yellow with the veins neatly outlined in bright ochre-yellow and brown. The upper sides of the wings have blacker markings.

HABITS & HABITAT A fast-flying, powerful and noticeable butterfly of drylands and semi-desert regions. Tends to fly fairly high and purposefully, but can also be found visiting flowering bushes (*Cadaba, Maerua*) and wildflowers. It pollinates several desert plants specifically adapted for butterfly pollination (such as *Gloriosa minor* shown here).

Purple tip
Colotis ione

~40mm A large, elegant, powerful butterfly with a wingspan of 55–60mm. The male has white wings with intense purple tips to the forewings. The female is similar, but duller and more variable. The veins on the undersides of the wings in both sexes are lightly outlined in black. The eyes are bright and mottled and the proboscis is well developed.

HABITS & HABITAT A common butterfly of savanna, grassland and bush after the rains. Most often seen visiting flowers, including fireball lilies (shown here), aloes and a number of other species. Flight is swift. Also spends time basking in sunshine.

Orange tips
Colotis spp.

~20mm Medium-sized butterflies with a wingspan of ~40mm. Variable, with slightly rounded, almost glowing orange- or red-orange-tipped wings. Females are duller and even more variable, with blackish markings on the wings. There is some seasonal variation. Head and eyes are fairly small.

HABITS & HABITAT Very common and widespread across East Africa in habitats from dry bushland to high-altitude areas. Most abundant in grassland and savanna. Often seen visiting wildflowers after the rains. Males are territorial, patrolling patches in search of mates.

Scarlet tip
Colotis danae

~20mm A medium-sized, bright, striking butterfly with a wingspan of 40–45mm. Male has white wings with scarlet wing tips. Female is darker with variable blackish markings on the wings.

HABITS & HABITAT A common, widespread and often noticed butterfly that has a lively flight pattern. Flutters actively between wildflowers,

pausing briefly to sip nectar before moving on. Can be found in large numbers on flowering bushes. Caterpillars feed on members of the caper family: *Capparis*, *Maerua* and *Cadaba*.

Magenta tip
Colotis celimene

~20mm Medium-sized butterflies with a wingspan of ~40mm. The males are among the most beautiful white butterflies found in East Africa. Their wings are dazzling white with rich, almost glowing, magenta wing tips and the veins are neatly outlined in black. Females are duller, without magenta wing tips.

HABITS & HABITAT A fast-flying, powerful butterfly that moves very swiftly and purposefully. Difficult to approach, as it is very nervous when on flowers. Engages in mud-puddling and sometimes pauses to rest on the ground. Found in drier habitats seasonally. A species typical of the Somali-Maasai centre of endemism.

Dark blue pansy
Junonia oenone

~25mm Medium-sized butterflies with a wingspan of ~40mm. One of the most beautiful and recognisable of East African butterflies. Wings are a deep velvety black with two bright, shiny blue circles on the hind wings (sometimes partly hidden by the forewings). Has red-and-blue eyespots and variable white markings on the edges and tips of the wings.
HABITS & HABITAT Perhaps one of the most familiar butterflies, as it is often encountered in gardens. Can be found sunning itself along paths and perched on flowers, where its beautiful colours and blue spots are unmistakable. Caterpillars feed on Acanthaceae.

Yellow pansy
Junonia hierta

~25mm A medium-sized, familiar, noticeable butterfly with a wingspan of ~40mm. The black-and-yellow wings have variable patterning, with bright blue spots on the hind wings. At rest, with wings folded, this butterfly looks very leaf-like and is superbly camouflaged.
HABITS & HABITAT Common and widespread during the rainy season, in drylands, grassland, savanna and bush. Often seen visiting flowers, including acacias and mass-flowering plants. Engages in mud-puddling, and is tame and approachable.

M.N. MUTISO

Little commodore
Junonia sophia

~20mm A pretty, rather small butterfly with a wingspan of ~30mm. Drab brown and orange in colour, but with intricate patterns. The veins are prominent, outlined in black. Can be highly variable. Males and females look similar.
HABITS & HABITAT Among the most common and widespread butterflies – ubiquitous in gardens, parks and cultivated areas across the region. Flight is fairly slow and fluttering. Pauses frequently to rest on leaves or flowers. Caterpillars feed on a wide range of plants, including *Justicia, Asystasia* and *Barleria.*

Jokers
Byblia spp.

~25mm Medium-sized butterflies with a wingspan of 30–35mm. Two similar, closely related species occur. Unmistakable with bold, strikingly patterned orange-and-black wings that are very eye-catching. Undersides of wings have silver-white markings.
HABITS & HABITAT Common and widespread butterflies in a wide range of habitats, but most frequently encountered in grassland, bush and savanna after the rains. They sometimes congregate around dung, bird droppings and other such delicacies. Flight is slow and sailing. Tame and confident, these butterflies are easily approached.

Eared commodore
Precis tugela

~40mm Fairly large commodore butterflies with a wingspan of ~55mm. One of several similar elegantly shaped butterflies. The wings are broad, with hooked tips, and are marked with a beautiful orange-pink band. However, the colour of this band varies with the seasons, and is sometimes yellow-orange (inset).
HABITS & HABITAT A fairly common butterfly in forest and woodland, as well as in cultivated areas in the highlands. Often found sunning itself alone in a prominent spot on a leaf or trunk. Slightly wary, will fly away, then circle and return to its perch. Caterpillars feed on *Plectranthus* and related plants.

Soldier commodore
Junonia terea

~25mm Medium-sized, dainty and familiar butterflies with a wingspan of ~40mm. Wings are variable shades of brown with a broad yellow band that runs the length of the wings and crosses both the fore- and hind wings.
HABITS & HABITAT A common and familiar butterfly of gardens, cultivated areas, moist bush and woodland habitats. Sometimes present in large numbers, visiting animal dung, patches of urine and flowers. Caterpillars feed on several common herbaceous plants including *Justicia*, *Barleria* and *Asystasia*.

False acraeas
Pseudacraea spp.

~50mm Large, beautiful butterflies with a wingspan of 65–75mm. This group includes a number of related species, all of which are stunning mimics of various acraea butterflies. Trimen's false acraea (*Pseudacraea boisduvali*), shown here, is one of the region's loveliest insects. Wings are rich orange and black, sometimes with pink or violet hues.

HABITS & HABITAT Fairly shy and wary butterflies that tend to fly high in the forest canopy and are difficult to approach closely. They soar confidently on outspread wings, occasionally settling at the edge of a stream to drink.

Forest mother-of-pearl
Salamis parhassus

~50mm Among Africa's loveliest and most memorable butterflies, these large insects have a wingspan of 80–95mm. The upper sides of the wings are a shining greenish-white, with oily violet reflections. The undersides are more muted. At rest, clinging to the undersides of foliage in the shade, they look like leaves.

HABITS & HABITAT Fairly common in forest and woodland habitats. Can be very abundant seasonally. They fly with a sailing motion. Often noticed in flight on sunny days, when their moving wings provide bursts of colour. They frequently settle on the ground to mud-puddle.

Blue mother-of-pearl
Salamis temora

~30mm Breathtakingly beautiful, unmistakable, large butterflies with a wingspan of 60–70mm. The upper sides of the wings are a deep cobalt blue with shades of purple and violet. The wings have an irregular outline with brownish edges. At rest, the undersides of the wings resemble dark dry leaves.

HABITS & HABITAT They are forest-dwelling butterflies of western Kenya, Uganda and western Tanzania, Rwanda and Burundi. Can be fairly common. Often encountered along forest trails or paths and at the edges of glades. They mud-puddle at the edges of streams and are attracted to rotting fruit, dung and carrion.

African map butterfly
Cyrestis camillus

~25mm A striking, pretty, medium-sized butterfly with a wingspan of 40–45mm. Easily recognised, it has white wings with narrow black and orange stripes. Has irregular, lobed wing margins and a prominent, angled tail.
HABITS & HABITAT Widespread in forests, especially rainforests, these butterflies are frequently encountered sunning themselves on muddy trails, where they can be rather nervous, often flying away and landing a short distance ahead with their wings held flat against the ground. The caterpillars feed on figs and *Zizyphus* spp.

Lurid glider
Cymothoe lurida

~30mm Medium-sized butterflies with a wingspan of 55–85mm. These elegant, bright golden-yellow butterflies are found in wet forests throughout the region. Males are bright, almost shining golden yellow to ochre-yellow. Females are larger, with brown wings covered with white spots.
HABITS & HABITAT These butterflies are typically encountered in forests, where they fly along trails and paths, stopping to sun themselves on foliage, with spread wings. Attracted to rotting fruit dropped to the ground by feeding monkeys. Found in the forested western regions of Kenya, Tanzania and Uganda.

Red gliders
Cymothoe spp.

~25mm Medium-sized, stunning and unforgettable butterflies with a wingspan of 40–50mm. Males are an almost uniform deep glowing red that appears to smoulder in dappled sunlight. Females are brown and white. The group comprises a number of closely related species, including Hobart's red glider (*Cymothoe hobarti*), shown here.
HABITS & HABITAT A butterfly of rainforests in the west of the region (in Kenya found only in western rainforests). Males are frequently found patrolling along forest paths. Can be bold, often perching obligingly on shoes or backpacks.

Painted lady
Vanessa cardui

~25mm Medium-sized (but variable) butterflies with a wingspan of 40–50mm. Common, familiar and widespread. Wings are a pretty pinkish-orange with white and brown markings. Colour intensity varies. Males and females look similar.
HABITS & HABITAT A cosmopolitan species and among the most widely distributed butterflies worldwide, the painted lady is a species that migrates in many regions. Most often encountered in open habitats, including gardens with flowers. Flight strong and powerful. Basks on the ground in the mornings.

Leopard fritillaries
Phalanta spp.

~25mm A medium-sized butterfly with a wingspan of ~40mm. A couple of closely related, similar species occur in the region. The wings are a rich orange, covered with fine lines and spots. Undersides of wings are paler, resembling a dry leaf.
HABITS & HABITAT A common and widespread butterfly in many different habitats, including gardens and cultivated areas. Sometimes occurs seasonally in very large numbers, and is attracted to streams, dung and damp patches of urine. Tame and confident, it can often be approached as it basks in the sun.

Admirals
Antanartia spp.

15–25mm Medium-sized butterflies with a wingspan of 30–45mm. A number of similar related species occur in East Africa. Pretty, elegant butterflies, most species are brownish-black with striking yellow-orange bands on the forewings and leading edges of the hind wings. Wings are sharp, with irregular outlines and short, pointed tails.
HABITS & HABITAT *Antanartia* admirals are typically butterflies of highland and montane areas, often found at the forest edge on mountain ranges throughout East Africa. Very fond of flowers, they can often be seen sipping nectar from high-altitude wildflowers. Males are territorial, engaging in fights with rivals. Flight is fast and powerful.

Blue-spotted charaxes
Charaxes spp.

~40mm Large, robust butterflies with a wingspan of 70–80mm. This group includes a number of closely related butterflies in which the males have elegant cobalt blue wings, with lighter turquoise, violet or sky blue spots and patches. Females are larger, drab brown, with white bands on the forewings. The edges of the wings are sharply serrated in both sexes.

HABITS & HABITAT Active, powerful butterflies often seen flying along forest roads at great speed. Males are strongly attracted to dung and rotting fruit, where they are easily observed and can be approached closely, if this is done slowly.

Club-tailed charaxes
Charaxes zoolina

~20mm Medium-sized butterflies with a wingspan of 35–40mm. One of the smaller charaxes species. Wings are strongly curved, with pointed tips, and there are elegant, clubbed tails on the hind wings. Males and females are seasonally polymorphic, with both yellow-ochre or brown (dry season) and pale greenish-white (wet season, inset) forms.

HABITS & HABITAT These are butterflies of drier areas in savanna and acacia bushland, where they are often seen flying furiously around the tops of hills (hill-topping). The caterpillars feed on acacias and other legumes.

M N MUTISO

Green-veined charaxes
Charaxes candiope

~45mm Large, robust butterflies with a wingspan of 70–80mm. One of the most familiar and beautiful butterflies of East Africa. A distinctive feature of this insect are the thick, bright green veins in the wings, which are especially visible when the butterfly is at rest with its wings folded. Upper side is yellow, orange and brown.

HABITS & HABITAT A common butterfly in gardens, woodland, forest and riverine habitats. Often seen patrolling along roads and at the forest edge. Flight is powerful. Easily approached when feeding from dung or drinking fermenting sap from trees.

Giant charaxes
Charaxes castor

~45mm Very large, robust, striking butterflies with a wingspan of 80–90mm. They have amazingly intricate markings on the undersides of the wings, while the upper sides are dark brown with yellow bands running down their length.

HABITS & HABITAT Widespread and fairly common butterflies that often engage in hill-topping. Males can be very territorial and aggressive, even chasing after swifts and swallows! They love dung, rotting fruit and carrion, where they are often found feeding contentedly and can be approached closely.

White-barred charaxes
Charaxes brutus

~45mm One of the most powerfully built butterflies, it has a wingspan of 75–85mm. The sleek, sharply pointed black wings have a single, broad band running along their length, which breaks into spots on the forewings. The undersides of the wings are exquisite and intricately patterned, as is typical of many charaxes.

HABITS & HABITAT A common and widespread butterfly that is often seen flying in forests, woodlands and gardens. Flies very fast and generally quite high, but settles to feed on fruit, carrion and fermenting tree sap. Males are territorial.

Guineafowl butterfly
Hamanumida daedalus

~30mm A fairly large, unmistakable butterfly with a wingspan of ~50mm. Has rounded, soft grey wings that are covered with black-edged white spots. The pale brown, very leaf-like undersides provide camouflage.

HABITS & HABITAT A common and widespread butterfly in bush, grassland and savanna habitats. Usually found alone; will bask on the ground with wings spread; in the evenings, folds its wings and is hidden. If startled, flies a short distance away, then rests. Often drinks at the edges of puddles or streams. The caterpillars feed on the leaves of *Combretum* spp.

Diadem
Hypolimnas misippus

~40mm Large, striking and recognisable butterflies with a wingspan of 50–60mm. Males are deep jet-black with large, circular, pure white spots on their wings. Females are near-perfect mimics of the African queen butterfly.

HABITS & HABITAT A cosmopolitan species found in many different parts of the world. Commonly encountered in grasslands, savanna, gardens and cultivated areas. Males are territorial and will patrol an area with their fast, sailing flight. Females fly like the model species with a slow, buoyant, sailing motion.

Regal swallowtail
Papilio rex

~60mm A large, elegant butterfly with a wingspan of 100–120mm. Among the largest of East African butterflies, this species is a mimic of the beautiful tiger butterfly. Has black wings with pale yellow spots and a chestnut patch at the base of each forewing.

HABITS & HABITAT A beautiful and striking butterfly to watch in flight. Found in highland forest and montane habitats throughout the region. Males often engage in graceful hill-topping, which is a distinctive behaviour. Mostly found flying in the canopy, occasionally coming down to sip nectar from flowering shrubs and creepers.

African mocker swallowtail
Papilio dardanus

~50mm Large, elegant butterflies with a wingspan of 75–80mm. Males are unmistakable – creamish-white with variable black bands and elegant tails. Females are mimics of various toxic butterflies including the African queen and *Amauris* spp. Have large eyes and a long proboscis for drinking from flowers.

HABITS & HABITAT Common and widespread in forest, woodland and riverine forest habitats. Sometimes found in gardens and in areas where citrus is cultivated. Was used historically in the study of the genetic basis of polymorphism by Sir Cyril Clarke, who then went on to unravel the Rhesus factor in human blood groups.

Green-banded swallowtail

Papilio phorcas

~40mm Large and unmistakable with a wingspan of ~75mm. Males have black wings with beautiful, broad, pale green bands and elegant black tails. In females the bands are paler green or yellow. Both sexes have large eyes and a long proboscis.
HABITS & HABITAT Common and widespread swallowtails of highland forest and woodland. Can be seasonally abundant. Males engage in mud-puddling and will also gather on stream banks and at piles of dung. They frequently visit flowers, including a number of species that they pollinate (like *Kleinia*, shown here).

Narrow green-banded swallowtail

Papilio nireus

~40mm Large, elegant butterflies with a wingspan of ~80mm. A number of similar, closely related species occur. Wings are jet-black with a shiny, narrow turquoise band across both fore- and hind wings. Underside is blackish-brown with variable lighter markings. Appear drab and leaf-like when at rest with folded wings.
HABITS & HABITAT Very common in forest, woodland and riverine areas after rains. Large numbers of males can often be found mud-puddling at the edges of streams. Common visitors to many different flowers. Their wings flash beautifully in sunlight.

Constantine's swallowtail

Papilio constantinus

~45mm Fairly large, with a wingspan of 75–80mm. Wings blackish with striking creamish-yellow bands and spots. Hind wings have well-developed tails. Underside patterning is similar, but more finely speckled.
HABITS & HABITAT Common and widespread in the coastal regions, but also found in the Rift Valley and isolated mountain ranges in northern Kenya and Uganda. Active; flies quickly along forest trails and roads. Often visits flowers for nectar and occasionally joins in mud-puddling.

Citrus swallowtail
Papilio demodocus

~40mm A large, pretty swallowtail with a wingspan of 75–80mm. One of the most common and familiar East African butterflies. Wings are dark greenish-black and covered with beautiful, pale yellow spots and speckling. There are multicoloured eyespots on the hind wings. Has a long proboscis for drinking, and large eyes.

HABITS & HABITAT Found in virtually all habitat types, including drylands, where it is present after seasonal rains. Common in gardens, where the caterpillars are sometimes a minor pest on citrus trees. Avidly visits dung and damp patches.

Angolan white lady
Graphium angolanus

~35mm A fairly large, beautiful swallowtail with a wingspan of ~65mm. Their black wings are covered with elegant white spots and patches. The undersides of the wings are a rich brown with red patches at their bases.

HABITS & HABITAT A fairly common and widespread butterfly of moist coastal bush, savanna and woodland areas. Usually present only after good rains. Can be found sunning itself on leaves. A powerful flier. The caterpillars feed on members of the custard apple family (Annonaceae).

Swordtails
Graphium spp.

~40mm Medium-sized to large butterflies with a wingspan of 60–70mm. Members of this group are distinguished by the long, elegant, narrow tails that extend from their hind wings. Colouring is generally black with blue-green or green stripes on the wings. Some species have tiny amounts of red on the inner hind wings.

HABITS & HABITAT A fairly common and widespread group of butterflies in coastal forest, woodland and riverine areas. Can be seasonally abundant, gathering in very large numbers near streams or at damp patches.

Pea blue
Lampides boeticus

~15mm A fairly large butterfly for the family, with a wingspan of 30–35mm. Very familiar and recognisable. Upper sides of wings are a pure, pale powdery blue; the undersides are white, with intricate light brown streaks.

HABITS & HABITAT Very common and widespread in a wide range of habitats, including gardens and cultivated areas. A global species with a truly cosmopolitan distribution. A minor pest – caterpillars may be found feeding inside the pods of green peas and other legume species.

Common zebra blue
Leptotes pirithous

~15mm A medium-sized butterfly with a wingspan of ~30mm. There are a number of similar, closely related species. Males are more uniformly blue above than females, with tiny tails and a black spot on the hind wings. Females are prettier, with speckled blue-and-white patterning on the upper side and intricate brown-and-white mottling below.

HABITS & HABITAT Very common and widespread in a wide range of habitats including gardens and cultivated areas. Can sometimes occur in very large numbers and often found visiting flowers and migrating locally after the rains.

♀

Small copper
Lycaena phlaeas

~10mm A small, compact butterfly with a wingspan of ~25mm. One of the most recognisable butterflies in the blues and coppers family (Lycaenidae). Wings are a rich metallic orange, with black spots. Undersides of wings are duller orange.

HABITS & HABITAT A localised but fairly common butterfly found in highland areas and on mountains throughout the region. Flies vigorously, often whizzing by in a blur. Males are territorial and will furiously chase each other about. The caterpillars feed on *Polygonum* and *Rumex*, in wet grasslands.

M.N. MUTISO

MOTHS AND BUTTERFLIES 133

Hairstreak
Hypolycaena hatita

~15mm Medium-sized with a wingspan of ~30mm, this is one of East Africa's loveliest butterflies. Males are bright, intense blue with long, wiry tails. Females are paler with blue-grey and white wings and long tails that flutter gently in the breeze when the butterfly is at rest.

HABITS & HABITAT These are typical rainforest butterflies that are usually found sunning themselves on leaves or flying up and down paths with their long tails flashing in the air. Pairs engage in beautiful, upward-circling courtship flights.

♀

Azure hairstreak
Hemiolaus caeculus

~15mm A medium-sized butterfly with a wingspan of ~30mm. Males are a pure, intense blue on the upper sides of the wings, with blackish wing tips and spots. The undersides of the wings (shown here) are beautifully striped with red lines on a soft grey-white background. Females are duller.

HABITS & HABITAT A species found in coastal woodlands and forests. Spends long periods basking on foliage, where it can often be approached very closely and observed. The tails and eyespots on the hind wings create a false head, drawing attention away from the real head and allowing for a quick getaway if attacked.

Saffron sapphire
Iolaus pallene

~20mm Fairly large butterflies (for this family) with a wingspan of ~35mm. One of the most distinctive East African butterflies. Wings are pastel yellow with black edging on the upper surfaces and black stripes on the undersides.

HABITS & HABITAT A widespread butterfly from coastal to savanna regions and on kopjes in grassland. Never common, but noticed where present, as it perches in, and often returns to, prominent spots. Spends long periods perched or basking. Can often be approached quite closely.

Scarlets
Axiocerses spp.

~12mm A group of small, stocky butterflies with a wingspan of ~25mm. Patterning variable, but always a combination of bright, almost angry red and black shades on the upper sides of the wings. The undersides have more intricate coppery tones, with silver spots.

HABITS & HABITAT Butterflies of woodland, savanna and bush, where they can be fairly common in the wet season. Males often gather at a prominent tree, termite mound or other landmark from where they make rapid territorial sorties. They feed on a wide range of plants, including acacias and other legumes.

Silverlines
Spindasis spp.

~12mm A group of small, robust butterflies with a wingspan of 25–30mm. Among the most distinctive blues. The wings are blue with variable barred lines on the upper sides, and the undersides are cream with brown, black and silver squiggles.

HABITS & HABITAT Fairly localised inhabitants of bush and savanna, especially where large acacias grow. They live in close association with ants (a feature of many blues), and their biology is poorly understood. The caterpillars feed on acacias and other legumes, while closely guarded by ants.

Grass blues
Zizina and *Zizula* spp.

~10mm Tiny butterflies with a wingspan of <20mm. Delicate and very dainty, with slender bodies. The upper sides of the wings are soft blue and grey; the undersides are grey, covered with white-ringed black dots.

HABITS & HABITAT Among the most ubiquitous of the blues. Found among weeds in a wide range of habitats including on lawns and in cultivated areas. Can be present in large numbers during the wet season. They tend to wave their folded wings slowly from side to side when perched on flowers.

Sawflies TENTHRENIDAE

15–20mm Medium-sized insects that hold their
wings flat over the back when at rest. Robust,
with relatively long antennae and a large
abdomen that is yellow or yellow-orange in most
East African species and contrasts with the
black head and thorax.

HABITS & HABITAT Adults move around fairly
slowly, perching on and investigating vegetation.
Found in woodland, forest and gardens. The
larvae feed on foliage and may be slug-like
or caterpillar-like, depending on the species.
Some species are pests that feed on cultivated
cabbage, kale and fruit trees.

♀

Braconid parasitic wasps BRACONIDAE

5–25mm Small to medium-sized wasps.
Often brightly coloured with black markings,
but are sometimes plain red or orange. The
females have characteristically elongated,
noticeable ovipositors.

HABITS & HABITAT Ubiquitous in most habitats
where the insects that they can parasitise occur.
The larvae develop inside the bodies of a host
insect, where the female wasp lays her eggs.
Host species include the caterpillars of butterflies
and moths, flies, beetles and aphids. Highly host-
specific. In many species the characteristic white
cocoons 'burst' en masse from the bodies of
caterpillars. Useful in biological control.

Chalcid wasps CHALCIDIDAE

~5mm Small wasps with robust bodies and
distinctive, enlarged, 'muscular' hind legs. Body
sometimes metallic, often brightly coloured.
Eyes red or iridescent blue or green.

HABITS & HABITAT Ubiquitous in all habitats
where their host insect species occur. Often
found perching on and inspecting leaves or
seed pods in search of hosts. They parasitise
a wide range of insects, including the larvae
of butterflies and moths (Chalcid wasps) and
bruchid beetles (Pteromalid wasps). Most
of these wasps are host-specific. *Dinarmus
magnus*, pictured here, is a parasite of bruchid
beetles that feed in acacia seeds.

Fig wasps AGAONIDAE

~1mm Minute wasps that look like tiny specks
flying around fruiting fig trees. Viewed closely,
their bodies are mostly black, and females (like
the one shown here) have very long ovipositors.
Males are small, brown and wingless.
HABITS & HABITAT Found in association with
fig trees (*Ficus* spp.), with which they have
co-evolved and of which they are specialised
pollinators. This wasp completes its life cycle
entirely within the enclosed flower (synconium)
of the fig. One of the most elaborate and
specialised plant–pollinator relationships known;
neither partner can survive without the other.
Some species are parasitic of the figs, which
they use for breeding; others are parasitic of
wasp larvae, on which they feed.

Cuckoo wasps CHRYSIDIDAE

5–10mm A small to medium-sized wasp with
gorgeous metallic green or blue-green colouring.
Robustly built with a hard, sculptured body.
HABITS & HABITAT Widespread where their
host species occur. Diurnal, active parasites of
other wasps and solitary bees, and often found
patrolling in the vicinity of their nests. They roll
into a ball when disturbed and the hard body
helps to resist repulsive attacks by host species.
The larvae feed inside the nest cells of host
species on both the host's stores of food and
the host larvae themselves.

Velvet ants MUTILLIDAE

10–20mm Small to medium-sized wasps
with bold red bodies and white-spotted black
abdomens. The bright contrasting markings are a
classic example of warning colouring. The female
is wingless and may be mistaken for an ant. The
male (pictured here) has wings and can fly.
HABITS & HABITAT Common and widespread
wherever their host species occur. Often seen
walking around confidently on the ground or
searching for the nests of potential hosts. They
parasitise solitary bees and wasp larvae, as well
as flies, moths and cockroaches. Females can
deliver a painful sting.

Tiphiid wasps TIPHIIDAE

10–20mm Small to medium-sized wasps with narrow, elongated bodies and distinctive long antennae. Their bodies are often yellow, with bands or stripes on the abdomen. The wings are clear or tinted.

HABITS & HABITAT Ubiquitous and common in forest, woodland and bush, wherever their host species occur. Diurnal and active. Opportunistically visit flowers for nectar. Can be very common at certain times of year. They parasitise beetle larvae in the ground, including those of tiger beetles.

Spider-hunting wasps POMPILIDA

25–50mm Medium to large wasps with robust black or brown bodies, shiny black or coloured metallic wings and long, agile legs. The legs are bright orange or yellow in some species.

HABITS & HABITAT Distinctive wasps that are often observed moving on the ground in search of prey. Move in a confident, jerky fashion, often pausing and flicking their wings. Adult wasps hunt and capture spiders (like that shown here) that they paralyse with their stings. The spider is then stashed in the nest, where the wasp larva feeds on it while it is still alive. Nests are typically burrows excavated in soil or sandy ground.

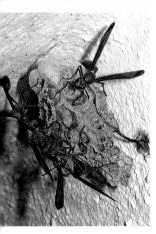

Paper wasps VESPIDA

20–40mm Medium to large wasps. Robustly built with large, triangular heads and eyes. Bodies long, with distinctive, thin wasp waists. Typically brown or red-brown, sometimes with yellow markings.

HABITS & HABITAT Ubiquitous and can be locally common in the vicinity of buildings or sheltered areas, where they construct their nests. Papery nests are made of chewed plant material and saliva and have multiple cells tended by several females. Larvae occupy nest cells singly and are fed with caterpillars. Adult wasps can be aggressive near their nests.

Potter wasps

EUMENIDAE

25–40mm Medium-sized wasps with a slender, elegant build and distinctive wasp waists that can be elongate in some species. Colour variable, often boldly coloured with brighter markings or patches of colour. Mandibles are long and curved.

HABITS & HABITAT Common and widespread, having adapted in many places to take advantage of man-made structures for nest construction. *Afreumenes* spp. construct dainty, pot-shaped nests from mud (both images). The females provision these nests with prey (often caterpillars) that are paralysed.

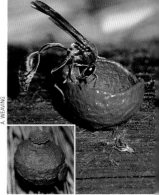
A. WEAVING

Large mud-dauber wasps

Sphecidae and *Delta* spp.

40–50mm Among the largest wasps in East Africa. Robustly built, with large heads, eyes and limbs. Bodies shiny brown, with red-brown legs and antennae.

HABITS & HABITAT Common in warm areas, where they are often found in association with buildings and will make use of sheltered walls and shelves on which to construct their nests. Curious and unafraid, will often circle people and enter rooms to cool down in front of fans. Their nests are constructed from wet mud and consist of multiple, stacked cells that are filled with paralysed caterpillars. Fascinating to watch at work during nest construction.

Beewolves

Philanthus spp.

15–30mm Medium-sized, robust, stocky wasps. Broad-headed, with large eyes. Colourful and striking, often with a bright yellow abdomen and legs and yellow markings on the body.

HABITS & HABITAT Common and widespread in gardens, woodland and bush. They are voracious predators that ambush honeybees, and sometimes seize other bee species foraging at flowers. Honeybees are stashed in underground burrow nests, where the developing larvae feed on them. Adult wasps also feed from flowers, where they are sometimes common.

Common carpenter bees   *Xylocopa* spp.
20–45mm Large, noisy and shiny black bees with dark wings. Some are all black, but most have bands of white or yellow on the thorax or abdomen. Some species are sexually dimorphic: the males are bright yellow or golden.

HABITS & HABITAT Found throughout East Africa in all habitat types. Important pollinators of crops (passion fruit, cowpeas, pigeon peas) and wildflowers. Active throughout the day, including mornings and evenings. Nests are tunnels bored into branches or old wood. Found near buildings where they are often noticed on verandahs. Males spend long periods patrolling a small territory.

Giant carpenter bee   *Xylocopa nigrita*
40–45mm The largest bee found in East Africa. The females are seen most often; they fly noisily and have distinctive black and white markings, with bands of white hairs along the sides of their abdomens. Males are bright gold.

HABITS & HABITAT Found in moist habitats including woodland, forest and savanna areas. Sometimes common on farmlands near natural habitat. Often heard buzzing loudly at the forest edge when visiting flowers. They are found at the flowers of most legumes, including cultivated cowpeas and pigeon peas. Females construct nests by excavating a tunnel in dead wood.

♀

♂

Small carpenter bees   *Ceratina* spp.
5–10mm Small to medium-sized bees. *Ceratina* are beautiful, distinctive bees with metallic colours on their bodies (typically green or blue), or they may be black with a few markings or bands. They have a fairly compact overall appearance.

HABITS & HABITAT Common bees, especially at the start of the rains, but even at other times of year, and can be found visiting a wide range of wildflowers and flowering trees. They tend to specialise on one kind of flower at a time, and can be observed around aloes in many dryland areas, where they collect pollen. Nests are excavated in pithy, dry stems, including the old flowering spikes of aloes.

Amegilla bees
Amegilla spp.

10–15mm Distinctive, with bright bands on the abdomen – white, yellow, orange or tan, but occasionally blue or iridescent blue-green in some forest and woodland species. The long tongue is often held out when feeding. Many different species are found in East Africa.

HABITS & HABITAT They fly noisily, with a high-pitched buzz, and move swiftly in jerky bursts between flowers. They are specialised pollinators of various species, including eggplants and tomatoes. Found in most habitat types including forest, woodland, savanna and bush. Seasonal in dry and semi-arid areas. They nest in tunnels excavated into the ground or a sheltered bank.

Longhorn bees
Tetraloniella spp.

10–15mm They are similar to *Amegilla*, but with distinctive, long antennae, especially in males. The thorax has brown or orange hairs. Bands on abdomen can be white, orange, yellow, tan or sepia.

HABITS & HABITAT Active throughout the day, especially in sunny periods and in the late afternoon. Fast and energetic in flight, visiting many different flower species, often members of the hibiscus family (Malvaceae) that open later in the day, including *Abutilon* and *Pavonia*. Their nests are tunnels excavated in the ground.

Nomia bees
HALICTIDAE

4–12mm A diverse group. Members have slightly elongate bodies and some species are wasp-like. Small to medium-sized, with bands of colour on the abdomen.

HABITS & HABITAT Seasonally abundant on wildflowers, acacias and most *Compositae*. Typically seen with bright white or yellow pollen patches on their legs. Many halictid bees can buzz-pollinate and visit specialised flowers to do so, including *Solanum* spp. They are important pollinators of cultivated eggplants in drylands. Their nests are tunnels, typically excavated in the ground or in a sheltered bank, and can be densely aggregated in favourable conditions.

Minute bees
Nomioides spp.

3–5mm Elegant and colourful, but easily overlooked due to their diminutive size. They tend to have yellow bodies, with dark stripes on the abdomen. Some species have greenish or metallic patches on their bodies.

HABITS & HABITAT Among the most common and active bees at wildflowers. They often forage in large numbers at flowering trees and wildflowers in drylands. Their nests are tunnels excavated in the ground and may be clustered in banks along roads, on the edges of dirt airstrips and in the walls of seasonal dams and pans.

Cuckoo bees
Thyreus spp.

15–20mm Medium to large, striking, elegant bees. They typically have bold black-and-white patterns or are black with light blue stripes. Their bodies are robust and very hard – adaptations for resisting attacks by their hosts.

HABITS & HABITAT As the name 'cuckoo bees' suggests, these bees are parasites that lay their eggs in other bees' nests. In East Africa their hosts are mainly *Amegilla* bees and other related species.Often found patrolling areas by flying low over the ground where their host bees nest, looking for an opportunity to sneak in and lay their own eggs.

Leafcutter bees
Megachilidae spp.

5–12mm A diverse family of typically medium-sized bees. Robust, with large heads and mandibles. Often have tinted wings. Pollen is carried on the underside of the abdomen, where it is often visible as a bright patch of colour.

HABITS & HABITAT Seasonally abundant, fast-flying bees that visit flowering herbs and trees, especially legumes (*Crotolaria, Vigna*), which must be 'tripped' for pollination to occur: the bees press down on a flower to expose the anthers and stigma. Important pollinators of cowpeas, pigeon peas and other crops. They cut sections from leaves, leaving circular gaps (hence the common name), then carry the cut sections to build tube nests or to line tunnels and cavities in dead wood, termite mounds or in the ground.

Honeybee
Apis mellifera

~10mm Active, noisy, familiar bees. There are two common subspecies: common honeybees (shown) are widespread and typical, with orange bands on the abdomen that grow darker in aged workers; mountain honeybees are slightly larger, with dark chocolate bodies, and are found only at high altitude.

HABITS & HABITAT Found across East Africa. Active by day, especially early in the morning in hot, arid areas. They visit a wide range of flowers opportunistically and are important pollinators of crops (coffee, passion fruit, sunflower, canola, runner beans). They carry pollen on their hind legs. Colonies comprise closely related sterile female workers, with a single, fertile, egg-laying queen and a few seasonal male drones. Can be aggressive near hives.

Small stingless (sweat) bees
Hypotrigona spp.

2–3mm Tiny, shiny black bees. Widespread, abundant and social. Often called 'sweat bees' in East Africa as they hover around humans on sunny days, sometimes entering the ears or nostrils.

HABITS & HABITAT Found from semi-desert to rainforest areas, at a range of flowers. They carry nectar and pollen in globs on their hind legs and take salts from sweat and from wet patches on the ground. They nest in tree cavities, constructing resin tubes. Harmless; widely exploited for honey.

Large stingless bees
Meliponula spp.

5–7mm Small, robust bees. Their bodies are orange or rufous, or may be black with yellow markings. The eyes are bright.

HABITS & HABITAT Typical of forests and woodland areas, in habitats that are not too disturbed. They visit a range of flowering forest trees including crotons, *Cordia* spp., and wildflowers at forest edges. They also visit fresh dung to drink salts. Can be shy when foraging. Their nests are found in large tree cavities and have a circular resin-lined entrance where workers gather. They are managed in hives in some parts of East Africa for their honey.

Black sugar ants
Technomyrmex spp.

2–3mm Widespread and abundant, they often enter and live in houses. Shiny black, fast-moving ants with bright, oval-shaped abdomens.
HABITS & HABITAT A ubiquitous 'tramp' species that benefits from disturbances to natural areas, where it takes a foothold alongside people. Often lives in houses or enters them to forage. Attracted to sugary foods and can also be found visiting flowers in gardens. Active both by day and at night. Colonies are located in large, diffuse nests underground or in cavities in walls or roofs. There are typically multiple queens, so colonies can cover large areas.

Harvester ants
Messor spp.

3–10mm Medium-sized, red to reddish-brown, with large heads. A colony may include both small- and extra large-headed workers.
HABITS & HABITAT They occur predominantly in grassland and savanna habitats. Important in dispersing the seeds of the dominant, widespread *Messor cephalotes* grass. They forage from visible trails that radiate from a bare, circular area around the nest entrance. Workers gather seeds and store them in underground chambers. Chaff from harvested seeds often marks the nest entrance. A reproductive queen lives deep in the nest. Similar species occur in woodland and forest areas.

Carpenter 'sugar' ants
Camponotus spp.

~10mm Medium-sized, active, diurnal or nocturnal ants. Long-legged, often with grey, silver or sometimes gold hair on the abdomen or body.
HABITS & HABITAT Ubiquitous and widespread in all habitat types, including high-altitude mountainous areas where few other ants occur. They forage singly or in small groups and occasionally form trails on tree trunks. They feed on plant nectar, scavenge for dead insects or fruit and tend insects for honeydew (especially on forest trees). Colonies are located in nests in the ground, the entrances to which are often marked by a shallow volcano-like crater of soil. A nest may contain several reproductive queens.

Safari ants (siafu)

Dorylus spp.

4–10mm One of East Africa's most legendary ants. Workers are bright red to red-black and highly variable in size, and include large-jawed, aggressive 'soldiers'. All workers are completely blind and eyeless. Males are the familiar large-eyed 'sausage flies' that are drawn to lights and disperse over long distances.

HABITS & HABITAT Found in forest, woodland and wet savanna, especially after rains. They forage en masse, both by day and at night, from heavily guarded trails. Voracious predators, they eat insects and arthropods, but also larger prey if they can subdue it. Prey is cut up into sections and carried back to a temporary bivouac, where it is fed to the larvae. Colonies are nomadic.

Singing ants

Pachycondyla spp.

15–20mm Large, shiny, grey-black ants that move in organised columns when hunting. Long-legged, large-eyed and agile, with large jaws. The queen and workers are of similar size and move together.

HABITS & HABITAT Savanna, grasslands and bush. Active primarily at dusk and dawn, when they leave their temporary nests to hunt. They follow trails laid by a scout to a termite mound, which they enter and raid, rapidly catching and killing termites, which are then carried back to the nest site. Occasionally they bring their larvae and pupae to the surface to air them out, especially after wet weather.

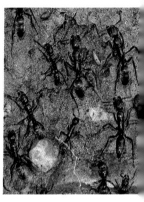

Polyrachis ants

Polyrachis spp.

~10mm Medium-sized black or grey ants with a hunchbacked appearance and spines on their backs. Slow-moving and not aggressive.

HABITS & HABITAT Found in forest, woodland and coastal gardens throughout the region. Most common in warm, wet habitats. Diurnal and gregarious, they can be found moving along tree trunks, twigs and branches, where they tend insects including membracid bugs, treehoppers and scale insects for their honeydew. Nests occur in dense vegetation, often constructed from detritus, or in a partial cavity.

SAWFLIES, WASPS, BEES AND ANTS   **145**

Cocktail acacia ants
Crematogaster spp.

~5mm These colourful, shiny black-and-red ants live exclusively on whistling thorn acacia trees. When alarmed, they will 'cock' the abdomen over the back, hence the name 'cocktail'. The red-headed cocktail ant (*Crematogaster mimosae*) has a red head and black body; the black-headed cocktail ant (*Crematogaster nigriceps*) has a black head and a brick red abdomen.

HABITS & HABITAT Diurnal, these ants inhabit the 'galls' (swollen thorns) of whistling thorn acacias. Entire colonies live on the trees and feed from the extra-floral nectary glands located on the leaves, on the honeydew derived from scale insects and on scavenged or captured insect prey. Aggressive when disturbed.

Skinny black acacia ant
Tetraponera penzigi

~5mm A shiny black, elongated ant, sometimes called the 'stiletto ant'.

HABITS & HABITAT Diurnal. Found exclusively on whistling thorn acacias, typically on smaller, older, battered trees. Shy and retiring, they don't respond when the tree is disturbed, although they can sting. They do not feed from extra-floral nectaries, but create a mesh of chewed plant material inside the 'galls' (swollen thorns) they inhabit. Galls resemble saltshakers, with many tiny, partially sealed holes on their surfaces.

Big-headed ant
Pheidole megacephala

2–3mm A small, often overlooked ant that enters homes and gardens. There are two kinds of workers: abundant individuals with normal-sized heads and some with larger heads, hence the common name.

HABITS & HABITAT Ubiquitous and spreading across East Africa. One of the world's worst invasive ants. Colonies are spread out over many square kilometres, with many thousands of queens. Nests are located underground and are often marked by loose detritus or remnants from foraging on the surface. These ants enter other ant and bee nests and quickly consume most other insect species that they encounter.

GLOSSARY

Alate The winged, reproductive form in social insects, including ants and termites.

Antennae A pair of sensory organs located on the heads of insects. Also known as feelers.

Brood ball A ball of dung rolled by dung beetles in which they lay their eggs and in which their larvae develop. The male rolls a nuptial ball for courtship.

Detritus Layers of rich, decomposing leaf, moss and other organic debris on old tree trunks or the soil, which typically provides a good habitat for insects.

Elytra The hard wing cases that cover a beetle's back, protecting its hind wings and body.

Endemic A species that is found only within a limited biogeographic region.

Furcula A forked organ on the end of the abdomen in certain insects, such as earwigs.

Gregarious Living together in groups, but not necessarily cooperating.

Hill-topping A behaviour for locating mates seen in flying insects, including butterflies and dragonflies. The males gather at the tops of hills in sunny weather to patrol, compete and wait for passing females.

Larva (pl. larvae) Immature form of an insect. This is typically the feeding stage that occurs between egg and pupa.

Lymphatic filariasis A disfiguring disease transmitted by mosquitoes; it is also known as elephantiasis.

Mandibles The jaws of an insect; their shape depends on the kind of food the insect eats and on its lifestyle.

Mate-guarding The process by which one individual, typically a male, protects or physically holds onto the female, so as to prevent her from mating with another individual. This behaviour is common in damselflies and dragonflies, some true bugs and flies.

Mating flight A behaviour engaged in by many ants and termites and some flies. Typically occurs at the beginning of the rains when swarms of winged reproductive individuals (alates) fly out in search of mates.

Model species A species that is typically unpalatable or has some other defensive feature that is mimicked by other insect species.

Mud-puddling Behaviour seen in insects, especially butterflies; they gather at damp patches (for example along streams or paths, including areas where animals have urinated) to suck up salts in the fluid.

Nutrient cycle The process by which nutrients, including nitrogen and carbon, are cycled through the environment. Termites are an important part of the nutrient cycle in Africa.

Omnivorous Feeding on both plant and animal matter. Some insects are scavengers of both kinds of food.

Ootheca The egg case of certain insects, including cockroaches (which carry it around) and praying mantids (which lay a papery mass on walls or trees).

Parasite An organism that consumes its prey in units of less than one, that is, on parts of or within a host's body. May be internal or external.

Parasitoid Organisms that develop inside the bodies of their hosts eventually bursting out and killing them. Some parasitic flies and wasps use this strategy.

Parental care Parental investment provided to offspring. Some insects provide parental care for their young – dung beetles, for example, tend brood balls underground.

Plasmodium The malaria parasite; it is transmitted by a vector, the malaria mosquito.

Sexual selection Natural selection in which individuals with a characteristic favoured by members of the opposite sex out-reproduce others in the population.

Shamba A small farm or garden area where crops or vegetables are grown.

Somali-Maasai centre of endemism An area that extends from the Horn of Africa south into Tanzania and that has a unique flora and fauna mainly adapted to dryland and savanna habitats.

INDEX TO SCIENTIFIC NAMES

INDEX TO COMMON NAMES